Resistance Fighter

A Teenage Girl in World War II France

RESISTANCE FIGHTER

A Teenage Girl in World War II France

by Elisabeth Sevier

with Robert W. Sevier

Edited and notes by
Richard A. Peters, Ph.D.
University of Central Oklahoma

Sunflower University Press®
1531 Yuma • P. O. Box 1009 • Manhattan, Kansas 66505-1009 USA

© 1998 by Elisabeth Sevier
Printed in the United States of America on acid-free paper.

Cover Art, French Flag, Jennifer Anne Barron, Edmond, OK
Design, Lori L Daniel

ISBN 0-89745-223-2

Technical Editor, Nancy Vesta

Layout, Lori L. Daniel

Sunflower University Press is a wholly-owned subsidiary
of the non-profit 501(c)3 Journal of the West, Inc.

For Colonel Adam, Alex, Andre, Annette, Charles, Felix, Geoff, Jean, Louis, Madame la Directrice, Marie, Michelle, Pierre, Dr. Soutille, and all the brave men and women — whose names I never knew — who served France as members of the Maquis *during the dark days of the Nazi occupation.*

If I live, I will fight, wherever I must, as long as I must, until the enemy is defeated and the national stain washed clean.

General Charles de Gaulle
Les Memoires de Guerre

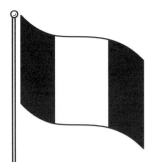

Contents

Dedication	v
Acknowledgments	xi
Introduction	xiii
Prologue	xvii
Chapter 1	1
Chapter 2	11
Chapter 3	20
Chapter 4	27
Chapter 5	39
Chapter 6	51
Chapter 7	64

Chapter 8	71
Chapter 9	82
Chapter 10	93
Chapter 11	100
Chapter 12	118
Chapter 13	125
Chapter 14	132
Chapter 15	137
Chapter 16	142
Chapter 17	147
Epilogue	151
Author's Note	171
Notes	172
Further Reading	177
Index	179

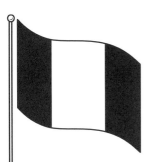

Acknowledgments

I AM INDEBTED TO Dr. Richard Peters and his wife Helen, whose support and encouragement have been vital to the completion of this book. Dr. Peters spent many hours editing the manuscript and researching the facts to place my Resistance activities in the proper historical perspectives.

I would like to thank Michelle Yelle, a graduate student of the editor, Dr. Peters, for her perceptive comments on the manuscript and for valuable research. I also am grateful to Ronald Joe Mitchell and Connie Schillingburg, history teachers at Edmond Memorial High School, who provided constant encouragement and support.

For 15 years, my French students have requested that I write about my experiences. I thank them for their interest and encouragement.

HYMNE de la RÉSISTANCE

Ami, entends-tu le vol noir
Des corbeaux sur nos plaines?
Ami, entends-tu ces cris sourds
Du pays qu'on enchaine?

Ohe, partisans pour veiller
les paysans c'est l'alarme.
Ce soir le pays connaitra
Le prix du sang et des larmes.

Montez de la ville descendez des collines camarades.
Sortez de la paille les fusils, la mitraille, les grenades.
Ohe, Franc-Tireur a la taille vos couteaux
Tirez vite.

The Hymn of the Resistance

Friends, do you hear the black flight
of the crows on our plains?
Friends, do you hear the mute cry
of our country in chains?

Hey, partisans watch over
the citizens it is to alarm.
Tonight the country will learn
the price of blood and tears.

Friends, come out from the cities, come down from the hills.
Bring out from the strawstacks the guns, the machine guns, the grenades.
Hey, partisans with sharpened knives
drawn swiftly.

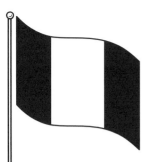

. . . A select few of the populace, found the occupation so intolerable that they felt compelled to act. French honor demanded they make some effort to oppose the Germans and hasten the day when France would be liberated from the oppressor. They did this by becoming dedicated members of the Resistance.

Introduction

ON JUNE 14, 1940, Parisians awoke to the crunch of German boots marching down the Avenue des Champs Elysées. This was the beginning of the German occupation, and a tragic chapter in the history of France.

The response of the French people to the occupation varied. Some became active collaborationists and took advantage of the opportunity to inflict vengeance upon the Republic they had always despised and, at the same time, to profit personally. Others, the vast majority, resented the Germans but accepted the occupation as a *fait accompli*, which they must endure. They knew that eventually the occupation would end, but until it did they must try to "get along" with the Germans and concentrate on their own survival. Although some of those in the second group eventually ended up in the Resistance, it was usually because they wished to escape the compulsory labor service in Germany. A third group, a select few of the populace, found the occupation so intolerable that they felt compelled to act. French honor demanded they make some effort to oppose the Germans and hasten the day when France would be liberated from the oppressor. They did this by becoming dedicated members of the Resistance.

In truth, one could belong to the Resistance in different ways, and after the war the Allied forces sometimes joked that it was almost impossible to meet a German *who had been* a member of the Nazi party or a Frenchman *who had not been* a member of the Resistance. Much depends upon how one defines "Resistance." A French postal official who purposely diverted mail from an important German official served the Resistance. The same could be said for railway workers who misdirected trains, printers who forged ration cards, individuals who concealed compromising papers, or those who carried messages at the request of Resistance leaders. The greatest risks, however, were taken by an estimated one percent of the population — the dedicated — who fled to the French countryside, joined the *Maquis*, and carried the war to the Germans.

Elisabeth Kapelian Sevier clearly belonged to the last group. Intensely patriotic, she found morally unacceptable the idea of "doing nothing" while the hated Boche carried out the Nazification of her beloved France. Other factors also made her a natural recruit for the Resistance. By nature a strong-willed teenager, she had an ambivalent but often unhappy relationship with her equally strong-willed mother, and thus, living at home was not without problems. In addition, the death of her physician father early in the war undoubtedly strengthened her bitterness toward the Germans. Elisabeth was quick to learn, attractive, boldly adventurous, and calm under pressure. These were useful qualities for members of the Resistance, and almost assuredly did not go unnoticed by its leaders in Paris looking for recruits.

Like so many members of the Resistance, Elisabeth began in a small way, carrying messages while working as a volunteer nurse for the Red Cross in Paris. Later, when the Gestapo became suspicious of her activities, in the early part of 1944, she was quickly escorted out of the city. Renamed Lisette, she became a member of the *Maquis de l'Etang-Neuf (Yonne)*. As a nurse, Lisette spent the next several months moving from one place to another with her unit, always trying to keep one step ahead of the Germans. During this time, she experienced the emotional ups and downs of a normal lifetime — anger, hate, sadness, joy, depression, and even love. As so often happens during wartime, she made close personal friends, only to suffer helplessly when they were tragically killed. Adventurous, she volunteered for dangerous missions aimed at derailing German supply trains and although captured, tortured, and wounded, Lisette survived and ultimately received the *Croix de Guerre,* one of the highest honors awarded by the French government.

Looking back after many years, the question may be asked, *What role did the Resistance play in the liberation of France?* It now seems clear that during the war the Allies were slow to recognize the potential value of the Resistance. No doubt, part of this may be explained by the difficulties encountered trying to work with so many politically divided Resistance leaders. Nevertheless, at the end of the war, it was clear that the Resistance had played a major role in the defeat of the Germans and had hastened the liberation of France.

In addition to their well-known role of providing critical intelligence to the Allied armies, Resistance units disrupted the German transportation system, protected the flanks of the advancing Allied armies by engaging isolated pockets of Germans passed over by the Allies, and frequently assumed political control of the towns and villages as the Germans retreated.

The French actually liberated large parts of their own country with very little help from the Allied armies, especially in western and southern France. Such achievements did not fail to impress General Dwight D. Eisenhower, Supreme Commander of the Allied Forces, who praised the Resistance forces in his memoir, *Crusade in Europe.* "Without their great assistance," General Eisenhower wrote, "the liberation of France and the defeat of the enemy in western Europe would have consumed a much longer time and meant greater losses to ourselves."[1]

Even if General Eisenhower's assessment had been incorrect, those who participated in the Resistance still played an important role in French history, and their sacrifices were not in vain. The Third Republic had for decades been marked by bitter internal divisions, followed by the German victory in 1940, which saw France defeated in a few short weeks. It was a humiliating time for the French, and the situation was not helped by the large number of prominent Frenchmen who cooperated enthusiastically with the Germans. The eyes of the world turned toward France and many wondered what could have happened to the nation, which only a few decades earlier had fought so gallantly at the Marne and Verdun. It appeared that the French had suddenly lost the will to defend their own country, even when invaded.

This story, however, is that of a young girl, Elisabeth, who was determined to fight back, regardless of the risks involved or the sacrifices she would be required to make. It is a personal, emotional story, told as accurately and faithfully as her memory will allow after so many years.

As a nurse, Elisabeth played a modest role in the Resistance. But when her role is multiplied by the many others who performed similar duties, that service assumes mammoth proportions. When so many leaders failed France, both before and during the war, it remained for individuals like Elisabeth to reclaim, by their actions, French honor and pride. These are precisely the people the British officer who trained special agents for the French Resistance had in mind when he wrote:

> No praise is too high for the courage of the anonymous people of France. They sought no rewards, no honours. They gave their homes and their lives, because, in their simple code of honour, their country demanded them.[2]

Dr. Richard A. Peters
University of Central Oklahoma, Edmond

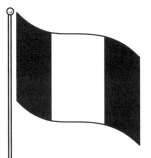

. . . I would be leaving Paris on a truck to escape the Gestapo. I was frightened and disoriented . . . .

Prologue

IT WAS A MOONLESS APRIL NIGHT, as black as pitch, in 1944 Paris, not far from the Arc de Triomphe. I was following the shadowy figure of a man I didn't even know, toward a truck, and then to an unknown destination. I was leaving behind my family, my friends, and my beloved Paris, all for a world that would be filled with hardships, sorrow, and terror. The Germans, however, gave me very little choice. The Gestapo had learned about my Resistance activities, and I could no longer safely remain in Paris.

The man I was following wore dark clothes and covered his graying hair with a black beret. I shivered as the cold night winds blew right through my body. I wished I had worn my heavy woolen sweater when I had left for work at the Red Cross, but it never occurred to me that I would be leaving Paris on a truck to escape the Gestapo. I was frightened and disoriented while walking briskly to keep up with the anonymous man ahead of me. Once I even stumbled and fell down.

We finally reached the truck and a friendly hand reached out of the darkness to help me climb aboard. A heavy canvas covering quickly dropped over the opening in the back. Inside, I could smell unwashed bodies and stale cigarette smoke. Someone pushed me to the side of the truck and I found myself sitting on a crude wooden bench next to another girl. She whispered that I must try to sleep and be very quiet.

"Where are we going?" I asked.

The girl replied that my questions would be answered later. Until then, we must do nothing to arouse suspicion. "If the truck stops, be as quiet as a church mouse."

As we drove into the night, I tried to settle down and make myself more comfortable on the wooden bench. I tried to sleep but my mind veered off in a thousand directions and sleep would not come. My heart pounded and I felt many emotions — anger, fear, guilt, excitement — all at the same time.

During the long night hours while the truck drove us farther and farther away from Paris, I think my entire life passed before me in my mind, almost like soldiers passing before a reviewing stand. *How did it ever happen*, I asked myself, *that I became involved with the Resistance in the first place?* Several million people lived in Paris, but only a very few actively participated in Resistance activities. The vast majority, it seemed to me, "adjusted" to the German occupation. They were unhappy with the Germans, but most still managed to go about their business as though life was normal, drawing as little attention to themselves as possible. I thought they were like ostriches that buried their heads in the sand. If they did not look, they could not see anything wrong.

My mother, Maman, I thought, was a little like an ostrich. She certainly did not like the Germans; very few French did. However, the Germans occupied the country, and Maman thought the only option for the French people was to cooperate and try to get along with them, regardless of how odious this task proved to be.

But I could never see how submitting to the Nazis could help my country or my family, and our different perspectives is one reason why Maman and I had so many problems. From the first time I saw the cocky Germans in Paris, I wanted them out of France. They were on *our* land, in *our* city, and they had no right to be. I disliked the Germans intensely. We called them the Boche, a derogatory word which means "thick heads" or "cabbage heads."[3] I just wanted to do my part to see they left our country as soon as possible. I was willing to give my life, if necessary, to liberate France.

But Maman was quite different, perhaps because she went through some very painful times in her youth. (I didn't know then that Maman had survived an Armenian refugee camp during and after World War I, where she lost a son and her first husband and endured much cruelty at the hands of her captors.) Maman didn't like to do anything risky.

When I was 15 years old, she even tried to persuade me to marry a man more than twice my age — a prominent businessman in Paris and a family acquaintance. I am sure Maman approved of him because she thought he would be able to provide me with economic security. *I would have a nice place to live and babies; what more could a young girl want?* Maman and I had bitter arguments over this man, and I finally won. I didn't want to marry anyone at that time, and certainly not because my marriage partner offered security.

Maman certainly suspected that I was involved in distributing underground newspapers or similar Resistance activities. This displeased her very much. She made this very clear to me the last morning I was home. "You are putting yourself and your family in too much danger," she said with her dark eyes flashing.

What could I say? I knew there was truth in what she said, so I refrained from making an angry retort.

I could never accept Maman's point of view about the occupation. I could not turn my back on my country and do nothing while the Germans turned Paris into another Berlin. The small acts I performed for the Resistance seemed so harmless and so easy as a Red Cross Defense worker. *No doubt about it*, I thought, *joining the Resistance was the right thing to do.*

Then, just when I convinced myself, I would think of Maman and my sister, Suzanne, and my eyes filled with tears. Even though Maman and I did not get along, I still felt a deep sense of sadness to be leaving home. *What would happen to them?* Maman had never quite been the same since Papa and my sister Annick died, and I felt she really needed me. *And what about Suzanne?* She absolutely adored and needed me. *What if the Germans did something terrible to her because of me?* The Germans were known to take families of suspected resistants to concentration camps for questioning. I prayed that the Germans would leave them alone and God would take good care of them while I was away.

I brushed away my tears and turned my face so that none of the others in the truck would see them. After all, they would only think of me as a crybaby. But even all this guilt and sadness did not prevent me from feeling a sense of excitement about becoming a part of a Resistance unit. Instead of watching my countrymen suffer one indignity after the other at the hands of the savage Germans, I would be fighting back. I would *show* Maman that the French people need not suffer humiliation; we could do something about it. We could stand up and fight, like the French army did at the Marne in 1914 when the Germans were stopped just outside Paris. We must fight like the French did during the One Hundred Years War, when Jeanne d'Arc led us to victory against the English.

I loved St. Jeanne. She had long been my idol and a great source of strength and inspiration for me. She symbolized so many noble qualities: courage, strength, love of country, and faith in God. All the French people, I thought, should look to St. Jeanne d'Arc for inspiration during this most difficult time when we had lost our freedom. She stood for everything good about my beloved France, and I prayed to God that I might be like her.

Maman, I thought, never really understood me and how I felt about things like Jeanne d'Arc. But Papa understood me much better. He was more patient and kind, and not nearly as domineering as Maman. Although Papa's busy medical practice didn't leave him much time for his family, when he was around he always seemed to have time to talk to me. We would discuss everything, and he often brought humor into what I thought to be a serious situation. Papa was my hero and I loved him very much. His death had left a huge void in my life.

And Grandmere, I thought, understood me better than anyone in the whole world. Like Papa, she was kind and patient. Like Maman, she possessed strength of will and character, but always exercised it gently rather than in a domineering way. I often wished Maman could be more like her. Although not much over five feet tall, Grandmere always seemed in control of every situation. Like Grandpere, she had grown up and lived in Russia until after the Revolution, when they both came to France. Grandmere, I believed, knew everything and could do anything. Highly intelligent and highly educated, Grandmere had been a professor at the University of St. Petersburg where she taught English. A career woman at that time, she could understand someone like me, who wanted to do more than get married and have babies. Whatever my dream, whatever I wanted to do, I could always count on encouragement from Grandmere. Her message was always the same: "If that is what you want to do, Elisabeth, you should try it." In nearly every way, Grandmere and I were kindred spirits, separated only by the difference in our ages. I worshiped her.

All these thoughts about my country and family kept turning over and over in my mind as the truck rolled on into the night. Slowly, the hours passed and I finally drifted off into a restless, uncomfortable sleep. Suddenly, the truck hit a rough area and I awoke with a jolt. By this time the darkness was beginning to give way to the light of early dawn, and I could see the shadowy forms of my companions. Five boys were sleeping with their bodies curled up or spread out in various forms on the truck bed and on the side seat. One snored loudly, like a badly tuned engine.

The other girl sat next to me and drowsed with her head resting on her chest. I closed my eyes and again tried to sleep, but without success. Restless and tense, I lifted the corner of the canvas and immediately saw the outline of tree skeletons against a breaking dawn. This brought a response from the girl, who punched my arm and whispered, "You are not supposed to do that." I instantly dropped the flap, but when I asked what harm looking out could do, she just closed her eyes and pretended to sleep.

All of a sudden, the truck lurched to a stop and everyone fell flat on the floor. *"Silence! Pas un bruit, ecoutez."* — *Quiet! Not a noise . . . listen* — one of the boys whispered. Everyone froze. I found myself holding my breath and sensed that the others were doing the same. We all knew German soldiers or French police would immediately arrest us if we were discovered. I heard voices outside but could not understand the words. Our driver must have known what to say because, after what seemed an eternity, the truck began to move and we all began to breathe again.

We continued our journey unmolested, driving in the daylight. I was tired, hungry, thirsty, nervous, and needed to relieve myself. I looked over my traveling companions, who by this time were all awake. They seemed to be about 18, perhaps a little older. However, I looked older than my 16 years. Maybe some of them were also younger than they appeared.

I wondered what events in their lives had brought them to this fate. *Were they fleeing to escape the mandatory service in the German work camps? To avoid arrest for their Resistance activities — or both?*

Starting in summer of 1942, the Germans offered to exchange one

French prisoner-of-war for three able-bodied French volunteers to work in German labor camps. Very few French volunteered, so the Germans resorted to a labor draft. On February 16, 1943, they introduced the Obligatory Labor Service (*Service du Travail Obligatoire*), or STO. While many in France complied with the new law, a vast number of deserters simply vanished into the woods and joined one of the *Maquis* units of the Resistance. *Maquis* literally, means "bush." Thus, to avoid forced labor in German factories and labor camps many French *Maquisards* "took to the bush."[4]

I wondered if I would be strong enough to face the challenge of being a *Maquisard*. I wanted so much to be strong and successful, like Grandmere or my heroine, Jeanne d'Arc. I hated the Germans. By the end of the journey, I knew fighting was something I had to do. Perhaps it was fate. Perhaps it was God's plan; maybe God had always intended that I join the Resistance and fight for the freedom of my country. This thought pleased me very much.

Whatever the reason, when I looked back on my life, it seemed many events portended such a role for me. This was especially true after the outbreak of World War II, when I begin my story.

. . . On September 1, 1939, Germany invaded Poland, and the terrible war, which would so much change my life and the lives of many others, had begun.

Chapter 1

I GREW UP IN PARIS — the City of Light — and to this day I say with great pride, "I am a Parisian." My name was Elisabeth Kapelian, and in 1939, just prior to the invasion and subsequent occupation of France by the German army, I was living in Paris with my family: Papa, Jean Kapelian, a family physician; Therese, my Maman, a housewife; Arthur, my brother, a 24-year-old university student; Annick, my sister, age 22, who was ill with tuberculosis; and Suzanne, my 8-year-old sister.

Our apartment was located at 89 Rue Rebeval, near the Parc des Butte Cheaumont, which is in the northeastern part of Paris. While we were by no means wealthy, Papa provided for the family very well. We lived in a nice apartment with the usual comforts of many other middle-class Parisian families.

I was 11 years old — not turning 12 until December. During the previous school year I attended the Catholic boarding school at St.

Germain en Laye, just west of Paris. During the summer, I was home with my family for two months and was very happy. I never really liked boarding school. I missed my family while away and disliked the strict discipline of the nuns.

We enjoyed a nice summer with family picnics and gatherings. I had plenty of time to spend with my brother, sisters, and the many cousins who often visited. I felt sad when the summer was almost over because I would soon be returning to St. Germain. When in school, I felt deserted and alone, often wondering why I had to attend the boarding school while my siblings were allowed to stay at home. It just did not seem fair.

On September 1, 1939, Germany invaded Poland, and the terrible war, which would so much change my life and the lives of many others, had begun. Two days later, France and Great Britain declared war on Germany. The war quickly became the chief topic of conversation within the household as Papa and my uncles gathered to talk about the probable effects the war would have upon their lives and to make plans to leave for the army. Maman and Papa had already made a decision to send Arthur, who had already performed his mandatory army service, to Marseilles to continue his university studies.

I returned to St. Germain in early September and gradually adjusted to my new friends and acquaintances. The prime topic of conversation at school was the developing crisis in Europe. Everyone talked about what the Germans would do next. *But why should we worry? After all, weren't we protected by the Maginot Line and our large army?*

I lived in a dormitory with approximately 30 other girls. The beds were lined up about two feet apart, and the nuns lived in private rooms immediately outside the dormitory room. All my clothes and possessions were in a trunk placed under the bed.

Everyone arose at 6 o'clock and went to Mass. But first, we had to wash up, make our beds, and clean our areas. The nuns always inspected to make certain we had completed all our chores properly before going to Mass. They ran the school very much like an army barracks and if everything was not as expected, they tore up the bed and instructed the girl to remake it.

After morning Mass, we went to the dining hall to eat with the 100-some students. We were all allowed to choose our own seats and we were served family style. Immediately after breakfast, class began, which we continued until noon, when we received a two-hour lunch break. After lunch, classes lasted until 4 o'clock. From 4 to 5 o'clock, we enjoyed ourselves in the courtyard and had an afternoon snack, usually consisting of a small piece of chocolate and a piece of bread. We were required to study from 5 to 7 o'clock in a supervised study hall. Between 7 and 8 o'clock, we were free to do as we pleased: to play, sleep, rest, read, or perform our daily housework. Dinner began at 8 o'clock sharp and we were back in our dormitory by 10 o'clock, when the nuns turned off the lights.

Each younger student was assigned a big sister, an upper-grade student who acted as a friend, a mentor, and generally performed the functions of an older sister in a family relationship. My big sister was Yvonne and she was of Armenian descent. She was a wonderfully kind girl who made my life at school much more bearable.

One morning in late September of 1939, Mother Superior, whom we called "Maman Seguin," called me into her office and informed me that my family had notified her that Papa had been called into the army. Maman would arrive soon to pick me up so that I could see Papa off at the train station. I felt very apprehensive because I had never really thought about how the war would affect my own family. I went to the dormitory, changed into my best dress, and waited for Maman to come.

Maman arrived about an hour later and we boarded a train for the short journey home. Her silence told me she was very sad. I kept questioning her about Papa: "Where was he going? When would he be back? Why did he have to leave?" I really do not believe Maman heard my questions. She just sat quietly lost in her own thoughts. When we arrived home, many of my relatives — uncles and aunts and many of my cousins — were there. They had prepared a dinner in the courtyard and we all sat down to eat. Afterwards, I played with my brother, sisters, and cousins until late in the evening and I actually forgot for awhile the reason I was home. After my relatives left, Maman put all of us to bed.

I then realized that Papa would be leaving the next day. I prayed the long night would never end, but my prayers could not hold back the dawn. At the first sign of light, I rose from my bed, dressed, and crept into the kitchen. Maman, dressed in black, stood at the sink rinsing dishes. She slightly scolded me for being up so early. I answered that I had been unable to sleep well because of worrying about Papa, and I wanted to go to the train station to see him leave. She agreed to let me go, but reminded me to be quiet so that I did not awaken my brother and sisters.

When the taxi arrived, Papa looked at me, smiled, and motioned me to come along. I ran to him and hugged him with all my strength. He patted me on the back and told me not to worry — he would be back soon and life would return to normal. This made me feel much better. I adored Papa, and after all, he was always right.

The first rays of the sun lined the clouds in deepest shades of pink and lavender as we left our apartment on Rue Rebeval. I breathed deeply and pointed out the beautiful sunrise to Papa and Maman. Papa laughed and said, "A sunrise is one of the most beautiful sights on earth, but it is a pity it happens so early in the morning when so few people are awake to enjoy it."

I tried to laugh at his attempt to be funny, but a lump filled my throat. No one spoke during the ride to the train station as we all were engaged in our own private thoughts.

We arrived at the station, which was packed with men in uniform saying good-bye to their loved ones. Most of my family who lived in or near Paris were also there to see Papa off. I looked away discreetly as Papa talked to Maman, but my eyes kept returning to them. Papa looked so handsome in his new uniform and almost as tall as Maman with his boots on. Maman, who had always insisted that a lady never showed affection or emotion in public, kissed and embraced Papa, then wiped tears from her eyes with her lace handkerchief. It was such a wonderful morning and I thought to myself: *How could the world look so bright and cheery when I felt so sad?*

The whistle blew and the soldiers began boarding the train. I knew Papa would soon be gone and wondered to myself: *How can I bear it?* I stood up very straight — to my full height — and reminded myself that young ladies of my age do not cry. Papa came over, picked me up, and hugged and kissed me. He told me I must be brave because he would be unhappy thinking of my crying and sadness. He also reminded me that the war would end quickly and he would be back with all of us very soon — Arthur, Annick, little Suzanne, and Maman. "You will see," he said. As he wiped my tears away with his handkerchief, I noticed that he, too, was crying. I looked into his beloved face, and felt a bond that nothing could ever erase. He sat me down, turned, kissed Maman, bid his brothers and sisters good-bye, and boarded the train.

The guard standing at the doorway called, "All aboard," the whistle sounded, and the train slowly began to move away. I started running along the platform shouting, "*Au revoir, Papa. Au revoir. Je t'aime. Je t'aime*

The Kapelian family, *circa* 1937: Suzanne (front), Papa, Maman, Elisabeth (top left), and Annick (top right). Arthur was not photographed because he was serving in the French army at the time.

beaucoup" — *Good-bye, Papa. Good-bye. I love you. I love you very much.* Papa shouted back while Maman called to him, reminding him to write. I could not keep up as the train picked up speed and so I stopped. Maman caught up to me, put her hands on my shoulders, and indicated that we needed to leave.

On that day, I think I felt the first real twinge of hate toward Adolf Hitler and Germany. I hated the Germans for separating my family, for causing my Papa to join the army and leave the rest of us at home. I didn't know that I would never see my Papa again.

On the way back to our apartment Maman told me that I would be staying home the rest of the week rather than returning to school. The ride home seemed very long and I thought of how the absence of Papa would affect all our lives. Maman was also quiet, but this was very typical of her — she was an intensely private person who seldom shared her feelings with anyone. She did not often engage in idle conversation, but when she spoke, we listened and heeded her direction and advice. The family, including my aunts and uncles, looked upon her as a person of great strength and iron conviction — a natural authoritarian. She was tall for a woman, standing 5 feet 11 inches, and generally wore her hair in a bun. Standing ramrod straight at all times and always dressed in black, Maman was an imposing figure. One could pick her out of a crowd very easily.

We arrived home and I spent the rest of the day talking and playing with my sisters. That evening, we had a late dinner and then gathered in the salon. The sense of loss within the family was profound. The atmosphere was contrived and strained, but my brother and sisters kept the conversation flowing by talking about their problems, desires, joys, and fears. I went to bed feeling more alone than ever; Papa and I had always shared a special kind of bond and I missed him terribly. *Where did I belong, to whom did I belong, and why did I have to live a life which seemed so bereft of the close family ties that I desired?*

Maman took me back to St. Germain on Sunday afternoon. Life for me returned to normal — to the routine I had practiced since beginning my school years. The Christmas season approached, but for reasons never explained to me at the time, I did not go home for the holiday. Indeed, the Christmas of 1939 was one of the saddest of my life. Many students stayed at the boarding school over Christmas in that first year of the war. The nuns tried, but failed to make our holidays festive. I finally went home for Easter in 1940 and while I was happy to be with my family again, home was not the same without Papa. We sat around, visited with relatives, spoke often of Papa, and made plans for what we would do when he returned.

In May of 1940, the sisters at St. Germain seemed to always be whispering in small groups. I heard enough to know that the German army had invaded not only part of France but our neighbors to the north: Belgium, Holland, and Luxembourg. In June of 1940, I was sent home. We were told nothing except that the government had closed the school temporarily and that it would soon reopen.

On the way home, I noticed that although passengers crowded the train stations, everything felt different: there were no smiling happy tourists rushing to see the wonders of Paris. Instead, the trains were filled with refugees fleeing from the Germans. Grim travelers with sad eyes pushed and shoved their way into the cars. Everyone seemed frightened and in a hurry. Panicked whispers took the place of laughter. Families stood in the station surrounded by bundles and baskets. It looked like everyone had packed in a hurry, taking all they could carry.

Every station the train passed looked the same. There was always a large crowd of people, most surrounded by their possessions, but some with nothing except the clothes they wore. I watched and wondered where they were all going. The sisters at St. Germain had been vague about why the schools were being closed. From listening to people on the train, I heard that German soldiers were on their way to Paris and everyone seemed to be afraid.

As the train pulled into the Paris station, I saw Maman standing on the platform. I flew off the train, yelled to her, and gave her a big hug. I could see she was preoccupied and clearly very upset. She grabbed my hand as I asked her what was wrong. She almost exploded, saying sharply that everything was wrong. "The Maginot Line[5] has fallen and the Germans are on the way to Paris. God only knows what will happen to us now." Then she reverted to her normal authoritarian manner, telling me to be quiet and not to ask so many questions. On the way home, she told me she did not know where Papa was and she had not heard from him in a number of days. Papa may have been taken prisoner or even worse.

I did not know how to respond, but I quickly replied: "Papa will be safe. After all, Papa is a doctor, not a soldier."

On June 10th, the French ministries and officials headed out of Paris on the road to Tours to set up the government. The French government remained at Tours until June 14th, when it moved to Bordeaux.

Parisians left the city by the thousands during the next few weeks. People crowded into the railroad stations to leave Paris before the Germans arrived, but Maman declared she would not be forced from her home by anyone. "Besides, we must stay here because this is where your Papa will come to find us," she said.

Maman did not tell us her primary reason for staying: Annick, my older sister, was very ill. Annick had suffered from epilepsy all her life. Dr. Montan had tried to get her frequent seizures under control but hormonal changes from adolescence exacerbated them. Dr. Montan thought she would adjust in time, but tuberculosis complicated control of the epilepsy. Maman had not confided in me; however, I learned about Annick's condition by listening to Maman and Dr. Montan talk.

On June 13th, notices were posted in the city informing the public that

Paris had been declared an "Open City" and would not be defended. The large numbers of defeated French soldiers descending upon Paris daily in advance of the approaching German armies spread further panic, and even more frightened French citizens took flight. Restaurants closed and shops were boarded up, making food hard to find.

The subways stopped running as workers abandoned their jobs to leave the city. The French commandeered buses, garbage trucks, sprinkler wagons, and any and all vehicles capable of taking them south — away from the Germans. Many people even left by bicycle. Garbage piled up and the streets became littered with broken furniture and forsaken possessions. The trains still ran, but could not accommodate the hordes of frightened people wanting to leave. The sky around Paris glowed from the fires of burning oil and gas stored in depots around the city.

As the city changed before our eyes, Maman tried to reassure us by telling us that we would be fine and home was the safest place to be. I felt in awe, having never witnessed anything like this in my short lifetime. I was afraid one minute and then reassured the next, but always wondering what would happen to us. To add to our difficulties, Annick's condition worsened. She experienced problems in breathing and began suffering several seizures each day. I spent most of my time reading and re-reading any books or magazines I could find or borrow.

One day while Suzanne and I were playing in the salon, there was a knock on the door. I opened it and found Aunt Celine. She asked for Maman, and without waiting for an answer, rushed into the kitchen where Maman was working. She informed Maman that she and Uncle Armand were leaving Paris and begged her to come with them. Maman replied that she could not go because of Annick's illness. Aunt Celine's eyes filled with tears as she told Maman that everyone was saying Hitler intended to destroy Paris. She and Uncle Armand were on their way to Marseilles to join my Uncle Antoine, and she pleaded again with Maman to accompany them. However, Maman never wavered and remained firm in her refusal. Finally, Aunt Celine had to leave, and after hugs and tearful good-byes, she departed. I was more frightened than ever and felt a real resentment toward my sister, Annick, for being so sick that we could not leave with Uncle Armand and Aunt Celine. I also blamed Maman for placing the interests of Annick above those of the rest of the family.

Darkness descended on the City of Light on June 14th as the Germans entered an almost deserted Paris and began their occupation. Two million people had fled in advance. The Germans confiscated most of the food and fuel, leaving Paris destitute. Most shops were closed or abandoned. Maman had previously depleted the few provisions she had managed to hoard, and there was not enough for all of us to eat that evening. This was the first time in my memory I had gone to bed hungry.

On June 16th, I awoke to a sound like thunder. I lay in bed and waited for it to cease, but it continued on and on. I ran into the salon and found Maman and Annick looking out the window onto the street. Maman put her fingers to her lips and pulled me up so that I could see outside. Hundreds of German soldiers in green uniforms marched down the street with their exaggerated goose steps. Their boots clattered as they struck the pavement and they were singing German songs. I could not contain my rage. The soldiers were responsible for the disruption of my life and the separation of my family. I cried out: "I hate them! I hate them!"

Maman abruptly let go of me, slapped my face, looked me straight in the eyes, and said, "You must never, never say anything like that again. This is dangerous talk and you will get us all into trouble if you talk like that. Promise me you will never say anything like that again."

I promised Maman. However, I told myself: *Whatever I could not say, I could still think.*

During the next several days, trucks rolled through the Paris streets with their loud speakers blaring out messages, telling Parisians to remain calm and orderly. Radio broadcasts informed us how the French regime had mishandled the government, and how much better life would be now that the Germans had arrived. Although the Germans that Parisians encountered on the streets generally acted polite and courteous, rumors abounded about people being killed with machine guns and bombs on the highways. We still had no food. *How could we trust captors who starved their helpless captives?*

Late one evening after the family had retired for the night, I woke up to voices and heard Maman crying. I slipped out of bed and crept near the salon where I saw my Uncle Armand, Aunt Celine's husband, sitting on the sofa. He was sobbing, with his head buried, while explaining to Maman how "they never had a chance."

While on the road to Marseilles, he had stopped the car to help an old woman reload a cart that had turned over. Suddenly, German planes appeared, bombing and strafing the people on the road. He looked up and saw his car explode, with Celine and their two sons still inside. Uncle

Armand kept repeating, "They are dead, they are dead Therese; I have nothing left."

Then he raised his head and looked at Maman with a grief-stricken and hopeless expression I would observe over and over again during the next few years. I silently returned to the bedroom without them ever knowing I had been there and cried myself to sleep. When I awoke the next morning, Uncle Armand was gone. Maman informed me of what had happened and said Uncle Armand had left to inform the remaining members of his family about the death of his wife and children. We never heard from Uncle Armand again. To this day, the family does not know what happened to him.

A short time later, we understood what had happened to Aunt Celine and the children. We learned through an underground newspaper account how thousands of fleeing refugees had effectively closed the roads. When the German army could not proceed due to the gridlock, the Luftwaffe was ordered to clear the way with bombs and machine-gun fire. After the first wave of planes passed, nothing remained on the roads except burning vehicles. Hundreds of French refugees died that day under German fire and thousands of others sought safety in ditches and fields.

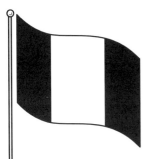

... Many French citizens were confused about who were the patriots and who were the traitors. It was all very sad. But then, at this time my beloved France was a very divided country.

Chapter 2

ON JUNE 16TH, Marshal Pétain replaced Paul Raynaud as the French Premier. On June 17th, the elderly hero of World War I spoke to the French people on the radio.[6] He offered his country "the gift of my person" to ease her suffering — he would lead France through all her difficulties. Pétain's announcement reassured some French and angered others.

Then he promised to seek an armistice with Germany to put an end to all hostilities, which was signed on June 22nd at Compiegne. Henceforth, France was divided into two zones. Northern France, including Paris and the coastline, would be occupied by the Germans. Southeastern France, the Unoccupied Zone, would be officially free. In reality, however, the armistice brought all of France under German authority.

Hitler diabolically signed the armistice on the exact site where Germany had surrendered to the Allies at the end of World War I —

the railway car at Compiegne, just northeast of Paris. On July 2nd the French government established its seat in the Unoccupied Zone at Vichy, where on July 9th and 10th the National Assembly voted to grant full authority to Pétain, effectively bringing an end to the Third Republic.[7] Our humiliation was complete.

At Vichy, Pétain and his corrupt, pro-fascist Premier, Pierre Laval, made many concessions and cooperated with the Nazis. Their treasonous actions led to their subsequent trial after the war where both were convicted by the French courts. However, in 1940, the majority of the French people still thought of Pétain as the "Hero of Verdun"; he carried enormous prestige and influence. No one in France was more highly regarded as a patriot than Marshal Pétain; whenever he spoke, France listened.

On the other hand, Pétain's brash and most vocal critic, General de Gaulle, was relatively untested and unknown, and his words had much less influence than those of Pétain. The same underground newsletter, *Combat*, that told the circumstances of Aunt Celine's death also printed General Charles de Gaulle's message to the French people, which had been broadcast from England on June 18th. France did not stand alone, General de Gaulle had said, and the "outcome of the struggle has not been decided by the Battle of France." He called the war a "world war" and said that everything needed to one day crush the enemies of France still existed. The General called on all Frenchmen on British soil to get in touch with him. "Whatever happens," General de Gaulle concluded, "the flame of French resistance must not and shall not die."[8]

Not long after General de Gaulle's speech appeared in the underground newspapers, we heard the General speak on the radio. Some of our neighbors were in our apartment at the time, and we listened attentively while he repeated many of the same things he had stated in his speech on June 18th. Our eyes became moist as we heard him tell us that the war was not lost, and that France would ultimately emerge victorious. After the speech, we kissed each other, and everyone agreed that France still had at least one true patriot. General de Gaulle had given us hope when we most needed it.[9]

Those of us who supported General de Gaulle knew we were in the minority, but still we could not bring ourselves to support the cheap, opportunistic policies emerging from Vichy. But the Pétain government denounced those who would continue to resist the Germans and branded them as traitors. When General de Gaulle refused to return to France as ordered by the Pétain government in June of 1940, he was court-martialed for desertion. On August 1, 1940, a military tribunal at Clermont-Ferrand condemned the General to death *in absentia*.[10]

Many French citizens were confused about who were the patriots and who were the traitors. It was all very sad. But then, at this time my beloved France was a very divided country.

In Paris, the Germans were clearly on their best behavior during the early weeks of the occupation. They walked the streets looking very much like tourists, snapping photographs everywhere, but generally respectful. Throughout the city, the Germans placed countless posters, all intended to persuade the French people to trust their new masters.

At the Arc de Triomphe, German soldiers even snapped to attention and saluted before taking pictures of the Tomb of the Unknown Soldier. German authorities clearly wanted Parisians to believe nothing had changed and life would go on as usual. In many ways it did, but no amount of German cunning and deceit could disguise the real differences that had occurred since the occupation. The curfew alone was sufficient to remind

One Nazi poster showed a kind and gentle German soldier helping a small French child.

Another German propaganda poster.

us we were all under German authority. At the time of the Armistice, the curfew was set at 11:00 p.m., after which all Parisians had to be off the streets unless they carried special authorization.

Fortunately, not everyone in France accepted the collaborative efforts of the Pétain government. Not long after the signing of the Armistice, the first acts of the Resistance began to take place, even though often trivial in nature. In Paris, anti-German graffiti began to appear. "Nazi Assassins" could be seen scrawled across German propaganda posters. These were small acts and no serious threat to the Germans, but were a sign that not everyone accepted the German occupation. The first resistants had begun to fight back, and the organized resistance would not be long in coming.

At that time, however, I was still only 12 years old, and left acts of opposition to others. Instead, my family settled into the routine of learning to live with fear and hunger. Obtaining food became a major problem — something quite new to us. As a physician, Papa had always provided sufficient income for the family to live and eat well. Now, with Papa in the army, our income was reduced to the small allotment provided by the government plus a supplement due to Annick's serious illness. Grandpere and Grandmere provided some financial assistance and vegetables from their garden. But since Maman had worked very little outside the home, she had no job skills to market. She was also needed at home to care for Annick. Everything considered, we had considerable less money to buy food than before the war.

But paying for the food was only part of the problem; the other part was finding it. When the Germans occupied France they seized a large part of the food supplies. Whatever remained was strictly rationed, and the government issued each French family a ration card. Without such a card one could only buy food found on the black market, which was extremely expensive.

As a consequence, each day Maman spent hours in food lines trying to obtain the meager rations that were authorized and available. Maman usually left the apartment early in the morning and did not return until late afternoon. There were three categories of food stamps: J-1 for babies to 4 years, J-2 for children from 4 to 12, and J-3 for those over 12 years of age. Most shops handled only one commodity at a time, which forced Maman to visit several stores, all with large lines, to obtain the food necessary for the family. It seemed Maman's entire life revolved around obtaining food. I can remember many times when I went to bed hungry.

I blamed all of these problems on the Germans and my hate for them grew each day. The mandatory blackouts every night in Paris only added to my frustration and anger. During blackouts, I frequently read in bed under the covers using a small flashlight to see the print. I loved to read and whenever possible I would lose myself in books. My imagination soared as on wings, and for a little while I became Jeanne d'Arc, Florence Nightingale, or any of my other treasured heroines. Momentarily at least, I forgot hunger, the Germans, and even Maman, if she had been cross with me.

The schools reopened in October 1940, and I returned to St. Germain. This time Suzanne accompanied me. Attending school served to mask the realities of war for us. We seemed far removed from the everyday problems that had plagued us at home. I found the school to be the same, with the sisters as strict as ever. Because food was so difficult to obtain, our meals were not as good. Our diet consisted of Jerusalem artichokes, beets, turnips, and rutabagas stewed together in a thin soup, sometimes flavored with a bit of meat. We wisely did not ask the source of the meat. When we received a package containing extra food luxuries from our families, like chocolate and jellies, the sisters required that we share with our classmates. I rarely saw or spoke to my sister because we were in separate dormitories, different classes, and we each had established our own friends.

One morning, Bridget, my best friend, and I were walking to the courtyard to play when we saw Sisters Louise and Veronica talking together. I motioned for Bridget to be quiet and then stopped to listen to what they were saying. They were talking about a student who had wet the bed twice during the week. Sister Louise, who I did not like because of her meanness and strict ways, was speaking to Sister Veronica about what could be done to remedy the situation. Sister Louise told Sister Veronica that the child needed a lesson in front of her friends to encourage her to be more careful. Sister Veronica disagreed and replied that the student probably could not help it. Sister Louise countered, "This is nonsense, the child is nine years old. Her mother has just spoiled her. We need to help her grow up, that's all."

Sister Louise picked up the soiled sheet that was laying near her and called, "Susie, come here." I then realized it was my sister they had been talking about. Suzanne came and greeted the sisters with a big smile, which immediately melted into a frown when she saw the sheet.

I shouted "No!" but Bridget held my arm and kept me from interfering. I told Bridget they just did not understand that when Suzanne's bladder became infected she could not help from wetting the bed. Bridget told me it would only make it worse if I interfered. "It will soon be over," she said, "and you can explain it to the sisters later."

Then I gasped as the sisters held the soiled sheet over Suzanne's head while her classmates gathered around and pointed at her, at the same time chanting, "Susie wet her bed, Susie wet her bed." Suzanne buried her head in her hands and her small body shuddered as she sobbed in humiliation.

I felt a surge of anger and ran over to pull the sheet away from the sisters, but they would not let go. I finally bit Sister Louise's hand until she dropped the sheet. I saw blood as she drew her hand away. Then she grabbed me by my hair and marched me off to Maman Seguin.

Everyone loved Maman Seguin. She had always been nice to me and had encouraged me throughout the school years to do my best. I waited outside her office while Sister Louise spoke to her. After a few minutes, Sister Louise came out and smirked as she motioned me to go into the office. I noticed with some satisfaction her hand was wrapped in a handkerchief.

Maman Seguin greeted me with sadness and asked why I had been such a naughty girl. I hung my head and said I was sorry to have disappointed her, but Suzanne's illness — tuberculosis — had caused her to wet the bed. She looked at me and said it was "an unfortunate incident," and she was not sure she agreed with the way it was handled, but it was wrong for me to attack Sister Louise. Then she asked if I agreed.

I lifted my chin and told her, " I had to make them stop because Suzanne was crying."

She replied, "Your loyalty to your sister is commendable, but you still must be punished." It would be necessary for me to spend the night in the *cave* — the cellar — and polish all the sisters' shoes.

It was just past noon when I went to the *cave*. I looked around and saw that the whitewashed plaster walls divided it into several cell-like rooms. A narrow cot and a wooden stool had been placed in one of the larger units. Dozens of shoes lined the shelves on one wall. I shivered from the damp and cold. A single bulb, dangling from the ceiling, provided the only light except for a small dirty window near the ceiling.

I sighed and counted the shoes to be polished. There were 52 ugly, black, high-topped shoes on the shelves. They reminded me of the horrible looking overshoes that Maman made me wear in foul weather. I checked the supplies: a stiff brush for cleaning, some rags, and two and a half pots of polish — not enough polish to shine all of the shoes. I would do the best I could with what was available. I picked up a rag and realized it was someone's worn-out underwear. I held it up to the light and giggled at the bloomers with a drawstring to tie around the waist and full legs extending all the way to the knees. I pictured Sister Louise wearing the ugly, inconvenient garment and laughed. *No wonder she was in a foul mood most of the time.*

I worked on the shoes the rest of the afternoon and only finished about half of them. The polish was almost gone so I used it sparingly, applying it only to the scuffed marks on the remaining shoes. The light from the tiny window had long since faded when Sister Veronica came down the stairs with my supper of watery soup and a small piece of bread. I informed her I could not finish because there was no more polish.

She replied, "Just do the best you can, our supplies are short." Then she paused and told me I could leave the light on only until I finished eating.

She smiled at me before reminding me to say my prayers and to go to bed early so that the night would pass more quickly. "Someone will come and get you in the morning for early Mass."

I tried to sleep, but kept hearing noises. I began to imagine terrible things, such as rats scurrying around, waiting for me to go to sleep so they could crawl up my cot and bite me. I heard noises and imagined someone was in the cellar with me. I was just too terrified to sleep, so I got up and started wandering around the cellar hoping to find something to read. There was nothing. I covered the tiny window with one of the old rags, turned the light on, and again began polishing shoes. I finally became so exhausted that I sprawled on the cot and fell asleep.

I awoke the next morning to the harsh voice of Sister Louise demanding to know why the light was still on. I was confused and disoriented, but replied, "I could not sleep so I finished the shoes, then fell asleep without remembering to turn off the light."

After inspecting the shoes, Sister Louise informed me that I did not do a satisfactory job. She added, "You must stay here until they are done properly."

I told her there was no more shoe polish, but she replied sharply, "The shoes must be cleaner; you will have to go over them with a brush, then rub them with a rag at the same time. Pray to God to make you a better girl." Then she turned and left.

I finally finished the shoes and waited for what seemed hours and hours. I watched the light fade at the small window and knew it was night. I became angrier and angrier at the injustice imposed by Sister Louise. Finally, I could contain my rage no longer. I took a container of whitewash used to freshen the walls and gleefully smeared it on the black shoes. I had almost finished when I heard a gasp. I looked up and saw Sister Louise standing with her arms folded, a stricken look on her face.

"What are you doing?" she shouted.

I defiantly answered, "Since you did not like them the first time and there was no more black polish, I was making them clean and white with the whitewash. You should be pleased," I told her.

Sister Louise's eyes narrowed and her cheeks flushed red. She called me a "bad, bad girl" and picked me up, raised my skirt, and spanked me. I tried to kick her, but to no avail. My hands went to my buttocks to soften the blows, but this accomplished nothing except to hurt my hands. Then I started screaming at the top of my voice, and Sister Louise finally stopped hitting me. I shouted to her that I would tell my parents of her cruelty. She told me: "Go right ahead — they are not here to help you anyway."

Once again, I was marched to Maman Seguin's office. My pride was probably damaged as much as my body. I certainly felt mortified. Maman Seguin shook her head and asked, "What am I going to do with you, Elisabeth? You are such a rebellious young girl. You will go far in life, *cherie*, but you must watch it. You are much too impulsive."

The words did not mean much to me then, but as time passed, they seemed to be prophetic. Maman Sequin did not send me back to the cellar but ordered me instead to wash dishes for the entire school for one week.

A few weeks later, school closed again and Suzanne and I were sent home. This was the last time that I would attend St. Germain. I shall always remember Maman Seguin with love and respect. I really felt the kindly Mother Superior was the first person, outside my family, to truly love and care for me. She was always kind and fair, and she helped me develop confidence through her faith in my abilities. I remember her advising me, "Elisabeth, do the best that you can and never give up."

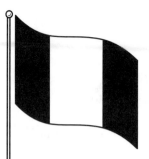

. . . After we had finished our evening meal, I heard a loud banging noise coming from next door. Someone yelled in German, we heard scuffling noises, then silence.

Chapter 3

WINTER SEEMED TO START EARLY towards the end of 1941, but then to me, it always appeared to be winter during the occupation. The cold and dark seemed to go on forever. Perhaps I noticed it more because I was home rather than in school. Daylight arrived late because all clocks had been changed to Berlin time.

Perhaps the winter seemed longer because the cold made me so hungry. The body requires more calories in cold weather and there was never enough to eat. The allowed daily ration was 1,200 calories per person, but Maman often could not get the full rations because of the shortages.

The discomfort, psychological as well as physical, of feeling dirty because hot water was unavailable added to our frustrations. The intense cold seemed to permeate my body. At least during the previous winter, I had been able to go to the church or public buildings to sit by the hot air registers. But the Germans used so much coal and fuel that there was little left for the French civilian population. Some banks and public buildings were still well heated, but citizens were carefully checked to make sure they had legitimate business at heated buildings and were not just trying to keep warm.

Maman spent much of her time trying to obtain enough food to keep our family alive. Frequently I watched Suzanne while Maman went shopping. Foraging took all Maman's energy, leaving her depressed and joyless.

I often felt bored and restless. I had read all the books in the house and the local library was closed. One day, while writing a letter to Bridget, I heard a timid knock on the door. I opened it cautiously, as Maman had taught me. A pale young man stood facing me, nervously crushing his beret with both hands. "Excuse me," he said apologetically, "but we are new here and I need a doctor for my wife who is having a baby and is in labor."

I told him I would try to find Dr. Montan who lived in the building. I sprinted downstairs and knocked on the doctor's door. Madame Montan answered, and I quickly told her of the problem. She answered, "Dr. Montan is out on a call, but I will try to reach him and will send him up as soon as possible."

I rushed back upstairs and rapped on the couple's door. The young man opened it immediately and his disappointment showed when he saw I was alone. I delivered the message from Madame Montan, adding, "Is there anything I can do?"

The small apartment was sparsely furnished with a few odds and ends left by its last elderly tenant, but it was clean and neat. A rickety chair and table furnished the living room. The apartment, originally designed as servant's quarters, had not been used for that purpose in my memory.

The young man, who introduced himself as Victor, led me into the bedroom. A pretty, dark-haired woman sat up on a pallet on the floor, clutching her enormous abdomen. Her face mirrored her apprehension and total concentration. After a moment she relaxed, looked up at Victor and smiled.

He took her hand and looked at her lovingly. "Denise," he said, "this is our neighbor, Elisabeth. She has sent for the doctor to help you and he will soon be here. She has offered to help until he arrives."

Denise looked at me. "How kind of you. This is our first baby and we are very far from home. As you noticed, Victor is very nervous."

I took a deep breath. Sometimes, looking older got one into trouble. I reassured her and told her not to worry, "Dr. Montan will arrive soon." I went into the kitchen and boiled water. Victor asked me why I was boiling water and I replied that I really did not know, but I had read books and watched movies and they always boiled water when someone was having a baby.

I returned to the bedroom and found Denise sitting upright, drenched in sweat, and obviously in great pain. She said, "It won't be long before the baby comes."

I picked up a clean rag by the bedside and wiped the sweat from her forehead. She informed me she felt a need to push down and this was the last stage of childbirth. I asked her, "How do you know?"

She replied, "My father had been a doctor and I had helped him." Denise stretched out on the pallet and opened her legs. I could see her stomach, which looked like a taut balloon ready to pop. I touched her belly with my hands. Denise grabbed my hand and squeezed, groaning loudly as her water broke. She then relaxed and breathed hard as if she had just finished a foot race. I looked up and saw Victor in the doorway. The look of concern on his face touched me deeply.

A pounding on the door startled us all. Dr. Montan hurried in with his black bag just as Denise began another contraction, declaring that he would take care of things now, and asked me to go into the parlor to comfort Victor.

I really did not want to leave, but a glare from Dr. Montan convinced me that I must. After reassuring Victor that the doctor had everything under control, I suggested we make coffee, but Victor informed me that they had none, only tea. I went to the kitchen and poured the hot water into the tea pot, leaving it to steep. Returning to the living room, I asked Victor, "How long have you been living here?"

"About a week," he replied.

A sudden scream caused both of us to jump. Victor ran the few steps to the bedroom, upsetting a small table in his haste. The cry of a baby stopped him short. He looked at me, smiled, and wiped tears from his eyes. I would never forget his look: a mixture of pride, joy, and fear.

Dr. Montan called out, "You have a fine baby girl." He asked me to please go downstairs and tell Madame Montan that he needed some help. I returned with Madame and helped her clean the tiny baby. Madame explained the purpose of the umbilical cord as we were washing the infant, then we wrapped her in a bit of clean flannel and handed her to Victor. He gingerly held her, seemingly terrified that he might harm her, while at the same time beaming with delight. Madame and I bathed Denise, changed her bed, and made her as comfortable as possible. Then we left the family to be alone in their happiness.

I ran home and rushed inside, excited and eager to tell Maman what had happened. She stood in the kitchen doorway with her hands on her hips. "Where have you been?" she demanded.

After I had told Maman all about the baby, she glared and reminded me that those people were strangers, and we knew nothing about them. "You could get us all into trouble with your meddling."

I turned and went into Annick's bedroom where she was sitting on the bed braiding Suzanne's hair. Suzanne's eyes were red and she sniffled as she related Maman's difficulties with a German soldier at the market. Maman had managed to buy three fresh eggs for our dinner when some people started fighting over food. The soldier ran over to break up the fight, but in the process knocked Maman down and broke the eggs. Annick added that we could expect nothing for dinner except the awful stew with the same old vegetables. "Maman couldn't even get bread, so she is in a bad mood, and we should give her a wide berth," she warned me.

Maman did not speak during dinner except to say that she would be leaving earlier than usual the next morning. The baker would give her an extra loaf of bread tomorrow, because she did not get any that day. Annick and I were washing and drying the dishes when someone knocked on the door. Dr. Montan and his wife brought a loaf of bread and a large hunk of cheese. A patient had given them more than they could eat and they hoped we would accept them. Maman took the food and thanked them for their kindness.

Dr. Montan then explained to Maman the events of the afternoon and told her that she should be very proud of me because of the help I had provided. Maman replied, "I am always proud of all my girls."

Dr. Montan turned to me. "You should consider a career in medicine, because you have a talent for it." I asked him about Victor and Denise, and he told me that they were doing fine.

Suzanne clasped her hands in delight and asked Maman if we could see the new baby. Dr. Montan picked up Suzanne and told her, "It would be best to leave them alone for awhile. The mother is tired and weak and it will be all she can do to take care of the baby."

Dr. Montan then asked Maman if I could stay with Denise the next day because Victor must be out most of the day. Maman replied, "I don't know this family and am afraid for Elisabeth to associate with them."

Dr. Montan soothed Maman by telling her, "They are just young kids in trouble, far from home, so they needed a little help. What harm could it do to pay them a few kindnesses?"

Maman thought about it. Then she said that I could look in on Denise from time to time.

After Dr. Montan left, Maman came into my room with a small bundle. "Elisabeth, I don't like this. These people could be in trouble with the law or with the Germans and it could get us all into trouble if we become involved with them. So be very careful and don't call attention to your visits." Maman stroked my hair in an uncharacteristic gesture of tenderness while telling me that these were sad times. We had to be suspicious of everyone, because our lives depended on caution and discretion. "Do you understand, Elisabeth?"

I replied that I did and I would be careful. Maman then handed me the small bundle containing Suzanne's layette. She asked me to give to it to Denise.

For the next several days I spent every spare moment next door. I became good friends with Denise and I loved taking care of little Marie. Victor spent a lot of time away from home trying to obtain food and supplies for his family. Because he was not registered in Paris, his only source of food was the black market. Dr. Montan brought them food whenever possible.

Denise breastfed Marie as long as she could, but her milk started drying up and the baby cried from hunger. I took part of Suzanne's milk ration to her until Maman found out and made me stop. Denise and Victor became more and more desperate to find milk to feed the baby.

When Marie was about three weeks old, a jubilant Victor burst into the room where Denise and I were taking turns holding the fussy and hungry baby. He shouted, "I have milk for the baby!" and held up his satchel. Denise threw her arms around him and they ended up on the floor, laughing like children. I watched their joy, felt a surge of relief, and then quietly left them to celebrate alone.

That evening, after we had finished our evening meal, I heard a loud banging noise coming from next door. Someone yelled in German, we heard scuffling noises, then silence. Maman gathered us in the salon and warned us to remain quiet. I wanted to go to see what was happening, but Maman held me tightly and told me in no uncertain terms that I could not leave.

Maman sent us to bed, but I could not sleep. I tossed and turned for what seemed an eternity. Finally, when I felt everyone else was sound asleep, I crept out of my room, opened the front door, and slipped out to check on my friends. Their front door had been nailed shut and a seal about five inches in diameter had been placed on the center panel. I could make out a red swastika with a warning to stay out. I pounded on the door, but there was no response. I started screaming for Denise. Maman appeared suddenly and clamped her hand over my mouth, telling me to be quiet or we would all be killed.

Maman pushed me into our apartment where I protested: "I heard something inside. Denise might need me."

Maman told me that the Germans had taken them away, probably because they were Jewish or enemies of the state. That was what I had feared, and I burst into tears and rushed into my room. I cried until there were no more tears, then fell into a troubled sleep.

Later that night, I was awakened by a faint sound. I bolted upright in my bed and listened carefully. I could hear the small cry of an infant coming from the wall which was next to Victor and Denise's apartment. I ran into the salon and told Maman: "They left Marie and I can hear her cry."

Maman came with me into the bedroom and we sat on the bed. We were very quiet and soon we heard the sound of a baby crying. Maman clamped her hand over her mouth and exclaimed, "What can we do? The apartment has been sealed."

I told Maman that I could crawl from our balcony to their balcony if she would help me. A space of about two feet separated the balconies with a narrow ledge connecting them. Maman got a rope, tied it to my waist in case I slipped, and I gingerly stepped on the ledge and onto Denise's balcony. It was actually very easy to do.

The balcony door was locked but the window next to it was open. I held my breath and climbed inside to Denise and Victor's bedroom. Though the pallet was unmade, nothing else seemed disturbed. It appeared that Victor and Denise had been awakened and apprehended while they were still in pajamas. Their day clothes were still neatly folded on a chair near the corner.

I found little Marie hidden in a small alcove in the kitchen. The precious evaporated milk lay beneath the padding in the box where she lay. I picked her up as she cried and put her in a bag that was in the kitchen. I carried her outside and carefully handed her to Maman, who was waiting on our balcony. Then I returned to retrieve the milk. Inside the apartment, I tried to leave everything exactly as I had found them.

Maman took Marie into our home and tried to console her. She asked me to prepare a bottle for her. Maman fed her and remarked how scrawny she was. She added, "We cannot keep her, because we cannot feed her."

I begged Maman to let us keep Marie, at least until she was stronger. "I'll take care of her! I'll take care of her!" I assured Maman.

Maman's face was soft as she held the baby and then warned me that no one must know Marie was with us. "No one, Elisabeth, do you understand?"

I nodded yes and Maman told me we would keep Marie until she filled out and a safe place could be found for her. Maman cautioned there would be no arguing when it was time for the baby to go. "You must promise," she demanded.

I smiled and promised.

We never again heard from or about Marie's parents, Victor and Denise. We always assumed they were sent to a German concentration camp, where they perished. No one ever returned to ask about Marie.

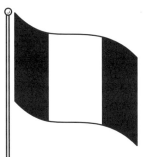

. . . On November 11, 1942, the Germans took over Unoccupied France. . . . All of France was under German military occupation, and any pretense on the part of the Pétain government to sustain French autonomy stood revealed as a sham for the remainder of the war.

Chapter 4

IN THE SPRING OF 1942 most Parisians were experiencing difficult times, but for a few months, our home was filled with joy. Annick and Suzanne bustled around helping me take care of little Marie. Even Maman smiled and hummed as she went about her daily chores. She started doing needlework again and showed me how to make simple shifts for Marie out of outgrown clothing.

Marie grew round and happy. She was a chubby, gurgling, laughing infant thriving in the atmosphere of attention and admiration and a source of joy to the whole family. But Maman worried constantly that someone would discover her and continually cautioned us to keep Marie quiet. She knew someone had told the Germans about Victor and Denise and she suspected Madame Sobel, the concierge.

As manager of the apartments, Madame Sobel seemed to be everywhere at once, lurking around corners and peeking through windows. She took pride in always knowing what happened in her building. She excused her nosiness by saying it was her duty to know what her tenants were doing.

One early spring day, as I was returning from a walk, I saw Madame Sobel standing in front of the door to our apartment with her hand cupped over her ear, listening. She whirled around when she saw me, then pretended she was picking something up from the floor of the hallway. I asked her if I could help in any way.

"Oh," she stammered, "I thought I heard a baby cry."

"A baby?" I replied, "What would we be doing with a baby?"

Then I heard a small angry cry. When Madame Sobel asked me about the noise, I just smiled and told her Suzanne was making the noise. "Annick is responsible for her care," I explained, "and since Suzanne claimed she is treated like a baby, she makes sounds like a tiny baby to irritate Annick." I put an annoyed look on my face to hide my fear that Madame Sobel would not believe me.

She stared at me with her watery blue eyes, her thin mouth set in a straight line. I felt a chill run through my body. Finally Madame Sobel smiled, but her eyes remained cold. "Thank you, Elisabeth, I have been curious about the sounds."

I told her that I would tell Suzanne to be quieter. Madame Sobel stood still for several moments, listening, but there was no sound from inside, so she turned to leave. I knew she would be back.

Annick was holding the fussy Marie when I walked into the apartment. She bounced her over her shoulder and crooned to her. The baby whimpered softly and drifted off to sleep. I told Annick that we must keep the baby from crying because Madame Sobel had heard her and had been trying to find out what was going on. Annick said she had been trying to quiet Marie but nothing seemed to work. I replied that we would ask Maman when she returned home, and I cautioned Annick not to inform Maman about Madame Sobel's suspicions.

Marie was still fussy when Maman arrived tired and discouraged from standing in the food lines. She told us that she had been unable to get milk for Suzanne. Annick and I looked at each other; we had been confiscating some of Suzanne's milk for Marie, and the evaporated milk was almost gone. Maman gave Marie some brandy with sugar and this caused her to drift off to a contented, restful sleep.

The next day, I staged a little show for Madame Sobel. Suzanne was told to play with her family of dolls in the courtyard. Madame Sobel always walked around the complex during lunch hour, poking into corners, and monitoring the comings and goings of her tenants. As Madame Sobel approached the courtyard where Suzanne was playing, Annick came rushing around the corner. "There you are," she shouted to Suzanne. "I have been looking everywhere for you. You know you are supposed to tell me when you leave the apartment." Suzanne started wailing on cue. I smiled as I watched from the balcony. Sounding remarkably like an infant, Suzanne stamped her feet, jerked her arm away from Annick's grasp and shrieked, "Leave me alone, you big bully. You are not Maman."

Madame Sobel stood and watched the exchange. Annick gathered Suzanne's dolls and grasped her hand to take her back to the apartment. Madame Sobel finally spoke, telling Annick that she was too hard on the child; Suzanne was almost 12 years old and needed a little freedom. Annick complied and told Suzanne that she could remain in the courtyard for awhile. Madame Sobel's thin lips curled into what passed for a smile as she moved on. I was elated and felt sure our little act had removed any doubts from Madame Sobel's mind about the noises in our apartment.

When Marie was three months old, Maman gathered all of us together around the kitchen table. We had just finished washing and drying the evening meal dishes. Maman cleared her throat and told us that for several weeks she had been trying to find a home for Marie. Finally, after pausing, she stated that she had located a good orphanage outside Paris.

Annick cuddled Marie and whispered to Maman, "No, no, please no." Suzanne burst into tears and I pulled her into my lap and tried to comfort her, through my own tears.

"Marie will be well taken care of," Maman continued. "They have a cow and some goats to provide fresh milk for her. Remember, I told all of you we could only keep her until I found a suitable home." Maman reminded us that we did not have enough food for ourselves, much less the milk required for a baby.

I looked at Maman and saw the pain on her face. I knew that giving up Marie would be as hard, if not harder, on Maman than on us. Maman took a handkerchief from her apron pocket, wiped her face, and announced in a slightly cracked voice, "Early tomorrow morning, I will be taking Marie with me when I go to the market." She turned and walked away, a clear signal that the subject was closed.

I was still asleep the next morning when Maman took Marie. True to my word, I did not mention Marie to Maman after she was gone.

A few days later, Maman had an unexpected guest. I can only remember her first name, Catherine. She had been one of Maman's childhood friends. Professionally, she was an opera singer, and sang minor roles at the Paris Opera. Catherine combed her shiny auburn hair in a style I had not seen before, and she wore absolutely beautiful clothes. I was fascinated with Catherine and thought her to be the most elegant woman I had ever seen. She gave us a small box of chocolates, which Maman immediately put away for later.

I came into the salon and asked if I could serve coffee. I wanted to be around Catherine as much as possible. Maman thanked me but said Suzanne was to have that honor; Annick and I were to stay in our room until we were called. I usually served guests, but because I had teased Suzanne so much, I knew Maman was punishing me. I hovered around the door to the salon, trying to overhear some of the conversation, but they were speaking so low I could only catch an occasional word. By concentrating very hard, I did manage to hear Catherine exclaim that the Germans were "pigs" but she was forced to be nice to them. I could not make out Maman's reply. Suzanne came in and served the coffee after which Catherine left.

I teased Suzanne about how long it had taken her to serve the coffee. I bragged that I could have made coffee three times and still scrub the floor in the time Suzanne needed to serve once. Suzanne's eyes filled with tears and I suddenly felt ashamed. I put my arms around Suzanne and told her that I was sorry. Then I went to her room and we played with her dolls, which seemed to make her happy.

Suzanne could not eat supper that evening because she became ill with a severe stomachache. After dinner, I went to her room to tell her a story and found her vomiting and doubled over with pain. Maman summoned Dr. Montan and he came immediately. He examined Suzanne and questioned her about what she had eaten. Suzanne kept saying she had not eaten anything. However, when I went to the kitchen to get a glass of water, I noticed a sprinkling of white granules on the floor by the shelves. Our two most precious supplies, flour and sugar, were stored in airtight containers on a high shelf, out of reach. Maman had carefully hoarded the sugar to be used only for special occasions.

I checked the sugar container and found it completely empty. When I whispered my discovery to Maman, she nodded her head and told Dr. Montan. He smiled down at Suzanne and told her she would be fine in a day or two. "Poor Suzanne has such a sweet tooth . . ." Maman explained to Dr. Montan.

As Maman walked Dr. Montan to the door, she asked him if he would give her some advice. Dr. Montan stopped and they went into the salon. I pretended to get a drink of water in the kitchen, but stopped outside the door and listened. I overheard Maman saying "She has too much energy and she is much too impetuous. She is going to get into serious trouble, I fear." I could not hear Dr. Montan's reply, but I felt sure that Maman was talking about me. I sensed I was a big problem for Maman.

Annick, always in fragile health, seemed content to lie around the house playing games with Suzanne and making up stories. I suspected Suzanne was not especially curious about things, but she was good-natured and generally happy. Perhaps that would change when she grew older. My sisters seemed content with life at home, as I could never be. But I went to sleep that night planning to be more helpful to Maman and to stop teasing my sisters.

Shortly thereafter, Maman came in after a long day foraging for supplies, looking exhausted. But she smiled when I appeared in the kitchen to help her put food away. "I have good news for you, Elisabeth," she said. "I have found a school for you. You will leave in two days to begin your studies again."

I protested that she would need me to help to care for Annick and Suzanne — both were sick with tuberculosis — but she would have none of that argument.

"No child," she replied, "Annick and Suzanne will be better soon and the most important thing is for you to continue your education."

I felt angry and rejected. I was sure Maman just wanted to get rid of me because she loved Annick and Suzanne much more than me.

I remained sullen and unusually quiet during my last few days at home. When the time came to leave, Maman took me to the train station to see me off. While waiting for my train, Maman turned to me and said she knew I did not want to leave, but it was best for me. "Someday you will thank me," she said.

I wanted to respond by denying it, to accuse Maman of wanting to get rid of me, but I knew she would cry if I said such words. And nothing would change, except more bad feelings would grow between Maman and me. So I just said, "*Au revoir*, Maman, I shall see you soon."

As I traveled to my new school, I began to think about what Maman had just told me. I realized she was right, that I was better off continuing my schooling, and that I would have never been happy at home without some stimulation. I needed to make new friends, examine new concepts, read new books, and keep my mind occupied with learning. Since beginning school, I had always been happiest while in a learning situation, when teachers challenged my mind and I could read and try to understand the mysteries and wonders of the world.

Once again, that September, I found myself in a Catholic boarding school — this time, St. Mary's. The school was located in south-central France, in the Unoccupied Zone, near the city of Bourges. It was in the Champagne Berrichonne country, a beautiful area with lakes and small hills with vineyards.

I adjusted to the new school easily, as I always did. The small school accepted only 35 students and was directed by the Franciscan Order. The school had no chapel, so we attended St. Mary's Church across the street every Wednesday and Sunday.

The routine was essentially the same as at any boarding school. We were required to go to confession every week. I was 14 years old, but I looked older. Many people took me to be 17 or 18.

Each time I went to confession, Father Dominique asked me unnecessary and suggestive personal questions. "Do you have a boyfriend?" he asked the first time I saw him. He also asked me if I had been touched in my private places by a man. I answered "no" to each question and wondered why it was any of his business. But he persisted in grilling me each time we met.

Finally, I asked Monique, my new best friend, if she had ever had Father Dominique as her confessor. She answered "yes," laughed, and then asked, "Has he tried to seduce you?"

I told her, "No, but he has been asking very personal questions."

"Watch out for him," Monique warned. "He likes young girls."

I grew to dread confession because Father Dominique became more suggestive each time. He began coming around to my side of the confessional, trying to touch me, but I stepped aside and rushed away. He would tell me what a pretty girl I was and that he could give me pleasure if I would let him. This was too much for me; I told him that I knew his behavior was wrong and asked him to please stop.

"No," he replied, "it is allowed because I am a man of God."

His reply frightened me so much that I went to see Mother Adele, the Mother Superior, and told her what had happened. She pursed her lips, stared at me, and said, "You are making a serious accusation.

"Many girls of your age have a vivid imagination," she added. "How can you be sure you are not mistaking simple affection for something else?"

I informed her that I was certain he had made advances to me.

Mother Adele ended the discussion by thanking me for coming to her, and promised she would consider what I had said.

I told Monique the story and she just laughed. "Last year," she said, "Father Dominique chased me all over the sanctuary." Finally she gave up and let him fondle her breasts. It was harmless. Monique suggested, "When Father Dominique serves as your confessor, leave and pretend you have finished."

I laughed, reflecting upon Monique's sophistication, and vowed to carry out her advice. However, after the Father Dominique experience, I found myself being more careful around priests.

I continued going to confession each week and Father Dominique continued to make inappropriate remarks. Each time he did, I just walked out after telling him: "Do not follow me or I will scream so loudly they will hear me in Paris."

Since I was leaving confession early, I could not immediately go back to school or the nuns would suspect I had skipped the confessional. So instead I walked to the back of the church and sat down on a bench in the garden.

One day while enjoying the sunshine in the garden, someone from behind me said, "*Salut.*" The voice startled me and I jumped up from the bench and looked around. I saw a young man sitting on his haunches, cultivating roses with a small trowel. He had blond, wavy hair and the bluest eyes I had ever seen.

He smiled and remarked, "I hope I didn't frighten you." When he stood up I could see he was tall and muscular.

And I, who was never at a loss for words, could think of nothing to say except, "*Salut.*" I wished I had worn my fresh white blouse and had combed my hair better that morning.

"My name is Norbert," he said, as he walked up to where I sat and extended his hand. Then he looked down at his hand, laughed, and withdrew it because it was caked with dirt. He wiped his hands on his gray knickers and sat down next to me. He asked, "Are you one of the girls from St. Mary's?"

I nodded yes, and told him that I had just come from confession and it had ended so quickly that I had time to waste before going back to school. The little garden had been so pleasant and inviting I decided to enjoy the spring sun on my face. Norbert agreed it was a pretty garden, and commented that he liked tending the flowers, especially the roses.

"Do you work full-time in the garden?" I asked.

He said that he also attended the boys' school next door. He went on to say that his brother, Father Paul, taught at the school. "Do you know him?"

I nodded and told him, "Father Paul is one of my favorites." (Actually, all of the girls liked him very much. They would sit and swoon, talking about how handsome he was and how disappointed they were he had chosen to become a priest.) "You look much like him," I added.

"Father Paul is like most big brothers. He likes to keep a close eye on his little brother," he laughed, as he moved a little closer to me.

I asked, "How did you learn about roses?"

He replied that his Maman always had a large flower garden and she had taught him to care for them. He also enjoyed going to his Grandmere's because she had a lovely garden with beautiful flowers.

I told him that I lived in an apartment in Paris and had never had the pleasure of tending a garden.

Norbert mentioned how exciting theater and opera must be in Paris. I agreed and told him how my Maman, Papa, and I loved music and the theater. My shyness disappeared after a few minutes and I learned that if I asked questions he would do most of the talking.

He was from a small village south of Bourges. It was in the mountains and there were a lot of pig farms in the area.

I laughed and he snorted like a pig, which made me laugh even harder. When he informed me that he once owned a pet pig, I thought he was teasing me but he insisted.

"We were never allowed to have pets," I said. I added that Maman considered them dirty, and they carried germs.

Norbert protested, "Pigs are actually very clean." He explained that they were more intelligent than dogs.

A bell rang in the distance, summoning us from our free time. I jumped up explaining that I must go; I had been away too long. Everyone would wonder where I had been.

"Can I see you again?" Norbert asked.

I told him that I would be back in the garden next week at the same time. I quickly ran across the street to my school.

The next week went by quickly. I spent a lot of time experimenting with my hair — trying to copy the style of Catherine, Maman's opera star friend. I thought I looked rather glamorous, but my classmates teased me about trying to look sophisticated. Besides, my dark, curly hair wouldn't stay confined. The curls kept escaping.

Monique guessed I had met someone from the boys' school. Her eyes sparkled as she informed me that communication between the two schools was discouraged. The boys were too young there anyway. She said that she preferred older men, at least 19 or 20, since she was almost 17. She offered to help me with my hair, advising me not to change it dramatically or he would know I liked him and was trying to impress him. Monique talked all the time she worked. When finished, she stepped back to get the full effect and exclaimed that I looked very grown-up. I surveyed the changes in the mirror and liked what I saw.

The day before I was to meet Norbert I shampooed my hair, rinsed it with vinegar, then added a touch of salad oil to make it shine. I pressed my clothes and polished my shoes. Just before leaving the next day, I would complete my preparations with a dab of Monique's perfume.

The next morning, Monique helped me to get ready. She said that my lips and cheeks were too pale and could use some lipstick and maybe some rouge.

When I told her that Maman would never allow me to wear makeup, Monique replied, "Well, we will not tell, will we?" She pinched my cheeks and asked me to bite my lips and look into the mirror. I was pleased with the results, and Monique told me how much prettier I looked when I had some color in my lips and cheeks.

Father Dominique served as my confessor as usual, but this time he was very businesslike. I finished confession, left, and hurried to meet Norbert. As I approached the bench in the garden, no one was there. I noticed a rose covering a small piece of paper on the bench. It was a note telling me that Norbert's schedule had changed and to please meet him before dinner at the chestnut tree at the side of the church.

My heart leaped with happiness as I went back to classes. I couldn't keep my mind on my school work the rest of the day. I found myself daydreaming about what I would say and how I should act when I saw Norbert again.

Norbert was waiting for me when I arrived that evening. He looked scrubbed and polished with his neatly combed hair and pressed trousers, but he seemed nervous. He smiled broadly when he saw me and asked me to sit down beside him on a stone ledge near the tree.

We sat together and our hands accidentally touched, shocking both of us. I laughed when I saw the look on his face and then he also laughed. The stiffness dissipated with our laughter.

Norbert told me that he was glad to see me again; he had feared I would not show up for our meeting. He explained that he had been given new duties as an altar boy and had been relieved from his duties in the garden, which was the reason he had been unable to meet me that morning.

Norbert said, "Some people expect me to become a priest like my brother." But he really thought this was unlikely. Then, grinning mischievously, he reached out and touched my cheek, which made a delicious shiver run through my body.

I told him that the priesthood was a noble profession, but I had always thought it would be very dull to be a nun or a priest. "They never seem to have any fun."

Norbert laughed, "I wouldn't go that far."

Time flew by as Norbert played me a tune on a harmonica that he carried in his pocket. I could see his expressive eyes dance as he watched me. We teased each other and laughed together. The bell rang, announcing supper, and we quickly made arrangements to meet again at the same time the following Sunday after the last Mass.

I danced through the rest of the week. I liked having a boyfriend, although I did not dare tell anyone except Monique. I smiled all the time and radiated such happiness that the sisters started taking special notice of me. They nodded with approval when they saw the change. I took more time with my appearance and seemed eager to attend Mass. Some of the nuns even talked about the possibility of my entering the convent. No one suspected that I was smitten by my first real relationship with a boy.

Early on Sunday morning, when we were dressing for Mass, it started raining. Since I had promised to meet Norbert near the chestnut tree, I began to think about an alternate site. I knew there was a small alcove on the opposite side of the church, protected by the roof overhang. It would be a perfect place to meet on a rainy day. I hurriedly wrote a note to Norbert, hoping to pass it to him when I saw him during Mass. Monique and I hurried to the church so we could get seats as near to the front as possible. We arrived in time to sit in the front pew.

Finally, Mass started and I saw Norbert, carrying the cross, precede Father Paul down the aisle. He saw me and winked, nodding slightly when he saw the note I was holding. The ritual continued and I watched for my chance. Norbert moved to assist the priest and came within a few feet from me. I tried to hand him the note, but he was just out of reach. He saw what I was trying to do and decided to assist me. While kneeling, he cupped his hand and placed it behind his back so I could place the note in his hand. But even this helpful maneuver did not allow me to reach his hand. Undaunted by this minor setback, I decided to toss the note. To improve my aim, I carefully folded the note into a wad. *At such close range,* I thought, *I could not miss.*

After waiting for the right moment, I lifted my arm and delivered my pitch. Unfortunately, just as I tossed the note, Monique jarred my arm and the note went flying through the air in a gentle arc. Monique and I watched in horror while the note descended directly into the chalice as Father Paul lifted the wine to his lips. A big purple stain appeared on his white robe. He looked around and had no problem identifying the two horrified faces in the front pew. He glared at us momentarily, then resumed Mass with his usual dignity. I don't remember much about the rest of the Mass.

As we left the church, Monique burst out in laughter, asking if I had seen the look on Father Paul's face as the note splashed into the chalice. I did not understand how she could laugh when we could be in serious trouble. Monique told me we should be happy that Father Paul had been giving Mass instead of one of the other priests. Most of them were old, stern, and "had no sense of humor whatsoever," she declared.

Sure enough, a summons came for me to appear at Father Paul's office at 2 o'clock. I felt I was walking to my doom. Father Paul greeted me and immediately inquired about my behavior that morning; he knew I had thrown a note of some kind into the communion wine. He held up a soggy piece of paper but admitted he could decipher only my signature. I felt that a great weight had been lifted from my shoulders. *Thank God he could not make out the rest of it.* I thought I detected a slight smile from Father Paul as he threw the wine-stained note into the waste container by his desk. He asked if I would enlighten him about the contents of the note. When I refused, he informed me that I must be punished for the disturbance, and assigned me a penance of 200 Hail Marys. He also made it very clear that my behavior was very inappropriate for the house of God.

I promised him it would "never, never happen again" and thanked him as I backed out of his office. I left positive I saw his smile and a twinkle in his eyes.

On November 11, 1942, the Germans took over Unoccupied France as a reaction to *Operation Torch*, the Allied invasion of North Africa, on November 8th. All of France was under German military occupation, and any pretense on the part of the Pétain government to sustain French autonomy stood revealed as a sham for the remainder of the war.[11] The occupation was a matter of deep concern for everyone in France, but especially for my family. My brother, Arthur, lived in Marseilles, as did many of my other relatives. After November 11th, they also lived and suffered under the German boot.

I did not go home for the Christmas holidays in 1942, but I was not as troubled as when I had missed the previous Christmas, perhaps because I enjoyed the smaller school more, and most of the other students also stayed during the holidays. I have fond memories of the time I spent at St. Mary's, and for the first time, I was really sad to leave when the school year ended.

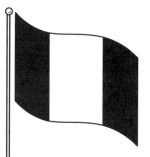

. . . Every day I found new reasons to hate the brutal Germans who ruled my beloved Paris. . . . Although I despised the intruders, I also feared them, and for good reasons.

Chapter 5

I RETURNED TO PARIS on a warm day in June of 1943, and Maman was at the station to meet me. I ran to her, gave her a big hug and kiss, and told her how much I had missed her. Maman seemed to stand there a long time just holding me tight. We took a taxi home, and on the way I gave her all the news about school and the new friends I had made at St. Mary's. I noticed the city looked very lifeless and sad. It seemed the Germans had drained Paris of its joys and beauty.

When we arrived at home, I sensed that something was wrong and I felt melancholy — unlike the other times when I had been so happy to return home to my family. Maman's letters had been strange of late: short, almost abrupt, and imparting little information. I wondered if I was really wanted at home. During my last stay at home, I had felt isolated, and this feeling of isolation returned.

Suzanne was her usual self, and she squealed with delight when she saw me. But all the drapes were drawn and the place looked dusty and unkept. "Suzanne, where is Annick?" I asked.

Suzanne looked sad and told me that Annick was in heaven.

It took a minute for the words to sink in, but the look on Suzanne's face told me it was true. "Maman! Maman!" I screamed, "Where is Annick? You must answer me!"

Maman told me to go to the salon and she followed me to the couch. She took me in her arms and told me that Annick had died in April while I was in school. "Annick was never very strong," she said. Dr. Montan did his best to save her, but he could not. Maman held me as we both cried. After a number of minutes, she composed herself and told me about how Annick had been seriously ill for weeks, especially her lungs which kept getting worse and worse. Finally, after so much suffering, she just did not have the strength nor the will to live.

"Maman," I asked, "why didn't you tell me? I could have come home and helped you."

Maman looked at me with her brown eyes and added that if I had been home she would have had to worry about one more mouth to feed. Besides, it would have accomplished nothing, since I could not have changed anything. I flinched at that hard remark from Maman, but I was also relieved to see that she had found her biting tongue again. It had frightened me to see her so passive and dispirited.

I went over to Maman, hugged her, and told her I knew she had been through a very difficult time. She drew her head up and said, "You just do not know, you just don't know."

I told her it would help to talk about it, but this remark upset her. Her eyes flashed with anger and she remarked sharply that if I thought talking would make the pain go away I was wrong. "Nothing can ever remove the pain," she said.

The war had seemed so far away when I was in school at St. Mary's. I knew that Maman had suffered greatly while dealing with Annick's illness, but I sensed her sadness went even deeper than the loss of Annick. *What more could have happened to make Maman so despondent?* Then I knew: Papa. I looked at Maman and cried, "Oh, no, Maman, not Papa! Has something happened to Papa?"

Maman's shoulders shook as she was wracked with huge, shuddering sobs. Then she told me that shortly before Christmas, the government had sent official notification that he had died, but gave no explanation. Maman continued by telling me how she went into a state of deep depression as she helplessly watched the family disintegrate before her eyes. "That is the reason you did not come home for Christmas this year," she admitted.

During the next few days I tried to concentrate on Suzanne, who was starved for affection. Together, we cleaned the apartment from top to bottom, and washed clothes and bed linens to stay busy and to keep our mind off our loss. Maman seemed locked in a private hell of her own, a world of sadness and loneliness that Suzanne and I could not penetrate. Suzanne probably missed Annick the most; after all, Annick had been her patient playmate and protector for as long as I could remember. I tried to take Annick's place and included Suzanne in as many projects as possible.

In late July, Maman stood in bread lines for two days without success. We were all hungry because bread had been the most nourishing and filling item in our diet. Maman said we had no money to purchase bread on the black market. The third morning, Maman awoke late and in a very angry mood because this meant she would not get bread again that day. The baker, whom Maman had known for years, had died two weeks before and the new man followed the rules rigorously. The first in line got the bread and when he ran out, no one got any. Maman came home more discouraged than ever.

I decided I must do something. I told Suzanne to get dressed because we were going out. Suzanne was more than willing to go anywhere; she seldom had the opportunity to leave the apartment area. We went to the street where I handed Suzanne a small bag, then we walked until I saw a cigarette butt. I picked it up while at the same time telling Suzanne to look for cigarette butts as well. We could sell our homemade cigarettes to buy food. I took one side of the street and Suzanne took the other. We approached a street where a number of German soldiers were hanging around a sidewalk café drinking beer. I told Suzanne, "This will be a fine place, because there should be plenty of cigarette butts."

While we were picking up the half-smoked cigarettes, some German soldiers noticed what we were doing and laughed. But I did not care — our bags were full. Just as we were getting ready to leave, a German soldier flipped his cigarette toward Suzanne. It landed in the folds of her dress as she was kneeling down to pick up another butt and caught her dress on fire. I ran to the nearest table, picked up a glass of beer and hurriedly threw it on Suzanne. The beer put out the flames and I brushed her dress to make sure the fire was completely out.

The German soldiers thought the whole incident very funny and they all had a good laugh. Then one of them looked at me and said in broken French, "Hey, pretty girl. Get rid of that brat and come home with me."

One of the soldiers who had not joined in the humiliation said something to the others in German which I could not understand. Yet, it was clear he was coming to our defense. He came over, took some change from his pocket and gave it to Suzanne, telling her to buy something for herself. Suzanne took the money and said, "Merci, monsieur." I grabbed her arm and dragged her away.

When we arrived home, Suzanne and I spent the next hour emptying all the tobacco into a pile from the half-smoked cigarettes. I carefully rolled the tobacco, using new papers, and took them to the vendor on the corner. He bought the cigarettes, and with Suzanne contributing the money from the German soldier, I had enough to purchase two loaves of bread and a rabbit from Madame Carpentier, the local dealer in black market commodities.

Maman had returned home by the time we arrived with some nice vegetables and milk. We had a wonderful meal that night, but Suzanne refused to eat the rabbit because she was convinced it was a cat. It may well have been a cat. During the first two years of the war the cat population of Paris disappeared at an alarming rate.

The long summer days began to wear upon me. I found it difficult to deal with Suzanne all day long and was bored thinking about nothing except household problems. Suzanne and I would take long walks. At least I was able to work off some nervous energy that way.

With so much free time on my hands, I began to look around for something to do. I could not sit around the apartment all day. Dr. Montan must have noticed I was restless; he mentioned a volunteer program at the Red Cross.

This idea appealed to me very much. I could learn to be a nurse, like Florence Nightingale. When I was about nine years old, I had read a book about this wonderful and courageous woman, and ever since I had wanted to become a nurse. Like Jeanne d'Arc, she became one of my heroines. Florence believed God had given her a special mission in life — to save other people. She and other nurses went to the Crimean War battlefields and saved the lives of hundreds of poor British soldiers who were not getting proper medical care.

Maman, for some reason, did not want me to become a nurse. "You should become a teacher," she said, "if you must pursue a career."

But I was very determined, and told Maman that no matter what she said, I intended to become a nurse and help people. So I applied to become a volunteer in the Red Cross, and was immediately accepted into the program.

A week later, I began my training. Every morning, I took the subway to the Red Cross Headquarters, located about a half-mile east of the Arc de Triomphe. Part of the training was theoretical and part practical. In the mornings I learned about the history and rules of the Red Cross. I also learned the theory behind the procedures I would perform in the field. I spent the afternoons training in local hospitals. Usually, I went to the Hospital Salpetriere, located on the Left Bank near the Gare d'Austerlitz. I traveled there by subway, which took me about 30 minutes. I learned patient care, first aid, how to take blood pressure, apply bandages properly, administer medicines, and stitch wounds.

As a volunteer nurse, I received no pay, but I found the work exciting and challenging. And I seemed to have a natural talent for nursing. I learned quickly, got along well with my fellow students and instructors, and felt fulfilled and proud to be doing something important to help my country. Moreover, I loved the freedom of being able to come and go from home almost as I pleased. As long as I had my Red Cross arm band on, the Germans let me come and go, even after curfew hours. My first taste of independence felt exhilarating as I rode my bicycle with its small motor assist — *Velo* — around Paris.

Every day I found new reasons to hate the brutal Germans who ruled my beloved Paris. I worked at being inconspicuous whenever the Boche were near. My usually perfect posture dissolved into a tired slump. I kept my head lowered and always avoided looking Germans directly in their eyes. Although I despised the intruders, I also feared them, and for good reasons.

Frequently, I took the train to Villeneuve St. Georges to my grandparents' home on the outskirts of Paris. Maman was always glad to see me go there because I would bring back word about her parents. One day, however, I witnessed an event that has been forever etched into my memory.

I was on the subway when three very drunken German soldiers boarded. I pretended not to notice them, but they were very loud, vulgar, and exceptionally rude to everyone nearby. I turned in my seat and pretended to sleep but their slurred, guttural speech grew louder and louder. Then I heard a shrill cry from a woman, and I turned around. I looked just in time to see a frightened young Jewish woman trying to hide her yellow star by holding her baby to her breast. The next thing I saw was almost as unbelievable as it was barbaric; one of the German soldiers drew his revolver and fired two shots at the mother and the baby.

I instinctively tried to get up and help, but an older man who sat next to me reached over and held me with his hand over my mouth. The subway pulled to a stop and as the doors opened, he pushed me outside. He asked me if I wanted to get myself killed. "You must learn not to interfere," he said. "There is nothing that you can do to help. Do you understand?"

I nodded numbly. I was shaking so badly I could not speak. Alone again, I somehow got home, although I could not remember the rest of the journey.

I always assumed the shots fired by the German soldier were fatal for the woman and the baby, but I never found out. I thought about the incident often, always hoping that they had somehow managed to survive.

During the next several weeks, I constantly found my thoughts returning to the terrified face of the young mother brutally shot in the subway. I could only forget when I stayed busy. At the Red Cross, I quickly earned a reputation for being an efficient worker always eager to help. I grew in confidence and maturity. Soon, I felt capable of handling anything that came up and my instructors encouraged me to do so.

One day in late 1943, as I left the hospital, a tall man in his thirties stepped out of the shadows and walked up to me. *"Tu vas vite avec ton velo"* — *You go fast on your bicycle*, he whispered as he stared into my face. His eyes were very piercing. He asked if I would do something for him. "Are you willing?"

I asked what he wanted of me. He answered, "Just ride to the Gestapo Headquarters and see how many cars are in the area. Count them without drawing attention to yourself and bring the number back to me."

I thought this an odd request, but decided that it would be quite harmless. I rode my bicycle a short distance to Gestapo Headquarters near the Champs des Elysées, counted the cars, and returned within a half hour. But when I returned, the man was gone. I shrugged and dismissed the incident from my mind.

Two days later, I left the hospital and headed toward my bicycle and heard footsteps behind me. In a loud whisper my contact said, "Don't turn around. Just slow down and I'll walk ahead of you." I did as he requested and he passed me quickly, whispering as he went by. Without acknowledging my presence, he asked me to give him the number of cars. Once again, I complied with his request.

The November chill had descended on Paris and the trees had already acquired the barren look of winter. One day my supervisor, whom I knew only as Madame la Directrice, called me into her office. She had noticed that I had not taken a day off in more than two weeks. I tried to protest, but she refused to listen to my arguments. She said, "If you work too hard you will begin to make foolish mistakes or take unnecessary risks. You are one of my best workers," she added, "and I intend to keep it that way." She instructed me to take two days off, go home, relax, and rejuvenate myself.

I left the building and walked slowly to my bicycle. *Two days at home* — how I dreaded it. Still, I peddled home and Suzanne greeted me with her usual squeal and a big hug. I asked her about Maman. Suzanne looked down at her hands and replied that Maman did not talk very much. Then she looked into my face and asked, "Elisabeth, why doesn't she like me?"

The pitiful look on Suzanne's face almost broke my heart and I pulled her close. I told her Maman loved her very much; she was sad because Annick and Papa had died. "One never forgets the loss of someone close," I explained, " and it will take a long time for Maman to recover." Suzanne gave me a big hug and told me she loved me because I always made her feel better.

My first day off was occupied with taking care of the many domestic chores I had neglected because of my busy schedule at the hospital. I cleaned house, arranged my clothing, and spent the rest of the day with Suzanne. More than once, the sirens signaled Allied bombing raids.[12] We had to spend much of the day in the subway, which we used as an air raid shelter.

My second day off work began quietly, but ended tragically. Around 6 o'clock sirens sounded again and we hurried to the subway. Suzanne dawdled, distracted by something she had seen in a shop window. As Maman and I yelled at her to hurry, a bomb hit the corner café near where Suzanne was loitering. Suzanne was caught in the shattering glass and splintering wood. Part of a beam hit her, bouncing across her shoulders and neck, and slamming her to the ground. When I reached her, she was unconscious and bleeding from head wounds. I could tell that both her shoulders were fractured. Maman screamed hysterically, but I focused all my attention on Suzanne.

Since I never went anywhere without my first aid kit, I was able to clean the cut on her head after brushing shards of glass from her hair. While her head bled profusely, the wound appeared to be superficial. I applied pressure to the wound for a few minutes, then turned my attention to the really serious problem, the fractures of her clavicles. I motioned for Maman to help me. Maman came over and wanted to lift Suzanne, but I cautioned her against moving her because of the fractures. I looked around to see if anyone else had been injured. There was no one except the shopkeeper who had suffered cuts on his arm from the flying glass. As I was bandaging his cuts, he informed me that he had called the ambulance for Suzanne.

Mercifully, the ambulance arrived before Suzanne regained consciousness. I could hardly swallow around the caustic lump of anger in my throat as we were transported to the nearby Hospital Tenon. As I watched Suzanne suffer in the hospital, I silently cried as I thought about how Hitler and the Germans had destroyed my family. Annick and Papa were already dead, along with my Aunt Celine and my cousins. Now Suzanne was hurt. *The senseless killing, the brutality, the hunger — it was all so pointless.*

I needed to do something to retaliate against the Germans, to stop the boiling rage inside me. While waiting in the hospital, I devised a plan, something I could do alone. The doctor said that Suzanne would be fine with no long-term effects, but I was still angry. As I left the hospital, I stopped by a table and stole a scalpel, then went home.

I asked Maman to cut my hair short, because it was always getting in my way. Maman found her scissors and began trimming away. When she finished, she stood back and seemed pleased with the results. A smile broke over her face as she remarked about the way my hair now curled around my face. I thanked Maman and told her that she should try to get some rest before we went to visit Suzanne again.

Ready now to carry out the plan I had conceived at the hospital, I went to Papa's room to select the proper clothes for my mission. I chose a black work shirt and trousers which were much too big for me. I made adjustments by rolling up the pants legs and the sleeves. Next, I put on a pair of Annick's ugly lace-up shoes, making them fit by wearing two pairs of socks, placed a black beret on my head and pulled it down over my short hair. Then I looked into the mirror; I definitely could pass for a boy.

After taking the best of Maman's paring knives from the kitchen while she was asleep, I went out. The November evening felt cold and damp. The wind kicked up fallen leaves, swirling them around playfully as twilight fell. I mounted my bicycle and headed toward the Gestapo Headquarters. When I arrived, I left my bicycle about a block away and slipped down the street to where the Nazi bicycles, motorcycles, and cars were parked. My heart pounded as I took the scalpel and began slashing the tires. Before finishing, I broke the scalpel and completed the job with the paring knife.

As I was leaving, I heard voices and the sound of footsteps walking towards me. I froze stiff as a statue next to a black car. A beam of light from passing cars scanned the vehicles. The footsteps grew louder and I could hear a woman speaking in French and laughing. Then the light from a passing car hit me full in the face and I found myself looking directly into the face of a French woman who was accompanied by a German officer. *Dear God*, I thought, *I've been caught.*

The woman, dressed in fur with a saucy little hat tilting across one eye, looked directly at me. Then she grabbed the German officer's arm and pointed in the opposite direction. They laughed and the woman put her arms around his neck and pulled him down for a passionate kiss. I felt as if I had been delivered. I released my clenched hand from the running board of the Citroen and quietly sneaked away. I owed my life to the French lady who had seen me, but had distracted the officer instead of pointing at me.

I retrieved my bicycle and began pedaling home. I felt scared, yet wonderfully euphoric and exhilarated as I inhaled the night air into my lungs. I had accomplished something important; I had hurt the barbaric Germans all by myself. I went home confident that Papa, Annick, Victor and Denise, Aunt Celine and her children, and all the other people who had been killed or injured by this horrible war would have approved my action.

I arrived home without incident, slipped into the apartment, and went directly to my room. I had not noticed Maman waiting in the dark kitchen.

"Where have you been?" Maman demanded to know as she stood in my doorway holding a flickering candle. Startled, I whirled around to face her. Maman gasped and asked me what I was doing in Papa's clothes.

I looked at her and told her she was better off not knowing what I did or where I had been. "Please don't ask me," I pleaded.

Maman knew I was involved in some sort of sabotage against the Germans. "You are going to get yourself killed," she said angrily, "and then my ruin will be complete."

I put my arms around Maman and tried to reassure her. I told her I had slashed some German tires, but that no one saw me and I had taken no chances. Even the horrible Boche would not kill me for that.

"You look like a boy, and you have the courage of a boy," Maman declared. "Your Papa would be proud of you, *cherie*." But then Maman warned that I must be more careful. "You, Suzanne, and Arthur are all I have left," she said sadly.

During the next several months I put my whole heart into thwarting the Germans at every opportunity. I gave out wrong directions and rode my bicycle in their path. These were small nuisance acts, but they gave my morale a big boost. It made me sad to see so many of my countrymen collaborate with the enemy. I began to hate the women who prostituted themselves to the Germans in return for food, furs, and jewels, while many others were forced to line their clothes and shoes with newspapers to ward off the cold.

I had a special hate for the *Milice* — the French military police — perhaps even more than for the Germans. The Vichy regime had created the *Milice* in January of 1943 to meet the threat posed, not only by the Resistance units, but also by the growing opposition among the French youths to performing mandatory labor service in Germany. It was headed by Joseph Darnand, a fanatical anti-Communist and fascist supporter, and assigned the task of rooting out the resistants.

These young French men, who trained as spies to uncover resistants and infiltrate Resistance movements, were frequently more cruel and vicious than the Germans. They were mercenaries, many recruited from the underworld.[13] They were paid handsomely for every agent they captured. And to receive their pay, they would prove to the Gestapo that they were every bit as cruel and repressive as the German squads.

In a cold, hungry country, like occupied France, anyone could be a spy. No one, not even one's closest neighbor, could be trusted. Even a family member might tell secrets to the Germans for a warm coat or better food rations. It was a world where people violated every principle and moral law they had been taught since childhood.

The bitter cold wind and snow of the winter forced most of us to huddle around makeshift stoves to stay warm. We could not get fuel, so we picked up every scrap of paper or splinter of wood we could find to provide a

The *Milice*, a Vichy French paramilitary police force that worked closely with the Germans in maintaining order, arresting Jews for deportation, and hunting down French Resistance groups. Notorious for its brutality, many Frenchmen feared the *Milice* even more than the dreaded Gestapo and *SS*.

small blaze for a moment of warmth. Babies and the older persons suffered the most, but everyone felt the cold and ever-present hunger.

One evening in early December, I received a telephone call at home from my unnamed contact in the Resistance. He had received information that a plane had crashed in the south part of Parc des Buttes Chaumont, near the Avenue Simon Bolivar. Because he knew I lived very near the park, he wanted me to go to the crash site quickly before the police and firefighters arrived. If the pilot was dead, he instructed me to take his name tags if I could safely do so.

I left immediately, going as fast as I could on my bicycle. As I approached the park, I could see clouds of black smoke, which guided me to the crash. I circled the burning aircraft and by its markings determined it was an American plane. Since no one had yet responded to the crash, I ran to the cockpit. Tragically, the pilot was not only dead but burned beyond recognition. I quickly took the name tags from the corpse and some scorched papers from the cockpit. The firemen arrived just as I was leaving the scene.

As instructed by my contact, I proceeded to a restaurant a few blocks south of the park on the corner of Rue de Belleville and Rue Rebeval. I entered the restaurant and saw only one couple sitting near the front and a waiter going toward the kitchen. No one even looked at me as I walked directly to the restroom in the back. Again, following his instructions, I lifted the lid of the toilet, placed the name tags in the tank, reinstalled the lid, and left the restaurant. On my way out, I overheard the waiter comment to someone that a nonpaying customer had just used the toilet. I didn't care; I had completed my assignment.

On the way home, I felt emotionally spent. Never in my life had I witnessed such a terrible scene. I thought about the young man killed in the crash and wondered who he was. I thought about my Uncle Iria, my Maman's youngest brother who lived in America and had joined the American army to help defeat Hitler. I prayed that he would survive the war; Maman had already lost too many loved ones. I also hoped the tags and papers I had taken from the burning plane would make it easier to identify the pilot and help notify his family. I felt very grateful to anyone who fought against the despicable Germans and helped the French people recover their freedom and independence.

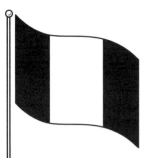

. . . From that moment on, I sensed the Gestapo watching me. . . . I continued to deliver packages, but Felix only gave me those that were small and easily concealed.

Chapter 6

MY MYSTERIOUS CONTACT appeared every week or two, each time asking me to perform some small task. I surmised that he served in the Resistance, and I wanted to be involved as well. In addition to delivering small packages, he used me to help warn Jewish Parisians that they were in danger of being discovered and arrested. He would give me an address, which I memorized. I would watch the address, often in an affluent neighborhood, to ensure that someone was home. Then I slid a blank, black envelope under the door, knocked three times, and left. The Jewish family understood the prearranged signal to leave.

I really never thought about how working with him could put my life in danger. But that changed one evening at the end of January 1944. I returned home late in the afternoon. I had been up all night, treating casualties during an intense bombardment, when someone spoke to me from behind. Jean-Claude, a neighborhood bully, stood smiling by his bicycle. "Race me to the alley," he said. "I have something to show you."

Although my instincts told me "no," I could not ignore a challenge coming from someone I disliked. Besides, by winning, I could take this smart aleck down a notch or two. "Just wait and see," I taunted, accepting his invitation. We were off and although I felt tired, my competitive nature took over and I reached the alley a bicycle's length ahead of him.

Once we were in the alley, Jean-Claude handed me a package, explaining he was delivering it for a man who had been looking for me. Then he gave me an address and asked if I would deliver the package. "Do you agree?" Jean-Claude asked impatiently.

The bundle, about four by eight inches, wrapped in brown paper and tied with twine, looked like some of the packages I had delivered before for my contact. "Of course, I understand what you want. I'm not stupid," I snapped back. I put it in my *mallette*, a small case, that held my Red Cross equipment and some personal articles, attached to my bicycle.

The frigid January day was sunny, but I could see snow clouds approaching from the north. Pedaling my bicycle kept me warm and I enjoyed a pleasant ride to the Bois de Vincennes, a lovely wooded area in southeastern Paris where many wealthy Parisians lived. I found the address easily and circled the building twice to make sure that it was safe to drop off my package. I saw a German soldier coming from the back alley of a big house, so I kept going. As I came around a third time, I met a German soldier on a bicycle. He started cycling after me and fear gripped my stomach like a vise. He shouted at me, but I could not understand what he was yelling.

I ducked into the woods and zigzagged through the trees of the Bois de Vincennes. The soldier had stopped yelling at me, but he was still in pursuit. I turned sharply, almost losing my balance as I hit an exposed root. I heard a loud noise and looked back to see that the soldier had lost control of his bicycle and smashed into a thicket of trees. He shouted at me and I knew he was cursing.

I tossed the packet into the woods and left the area as quickly as I could peddle. I passed two more German soldiers as I cycled out, but they were involved in conversation and barely looked up. A loud explosion came from the same area where I had thrown the package. *Had I been carrying a bomb?* My body shook so hard that I could hardly keep pedaling.

I reached home and went straight to bed, covering my shivering body with all my spare quilts. *Why would my contact risk my life by giving me explosives to carry?*

The next day, my contact met me outside the Red Cross Headquarters with a similar package. I demanded to know what it contained. "The last one contained explosives, I am sure of it," I told him.

He pulled me aside and harshly asked me what I was talking about; he had never given me explosives. I explained how Jean-Claude had given the package to me and asked me to deliver it.

Again he firmly denied asking a third person to contact me. "You shouldn't take anything from anyone except me, unless I myself direct it. Do you understand?"

I nodded my head yes as I swallowed hard. "I understand," I replied, "but if you trust me, you must tell me your name."

He smiled ruefully as he shook his head. "In this line of work, we trust no one," he said. "But you may call me Felix if you need to call me something. You must be careful; trust no one, not even those you know."

From that moment on, I sensed the Gestapo watching me. Though scared, I was also very pleased — the fear made me feel that I was helping France. During the next several weeks I continued to deliver packages, but Felix only gave me those that were small and easily concealed. One day he gave me a small note wrapped in waxed paper, to be carried in my mouth. If stopped by the Germans, I was to swallow it. I completed the mission without incident.

One morning in early April, I awoke when I heard someone outside the apartment door. I opened the door and found a large package which I pulled into the hallway and opened. The bundle contained copies of *Combat* and a note with only one word, "Distribute."

Anger gave me the energy to pack the newspapers in my *mallette* and take them several blocks away to dump them. It took me two trips. Since Felix had not contacted me, I could only assume that someone else had put the package there. If the newspapers had been discovered in our apartment, my entire family would have been in grave danger. Resistants who printed or distributed underground newspapers were often murdered.

The next afternoon, my supervisor, Madame la Directrice, called me aside and told me Maman had called and seemed determined to reach me. Then, after lowering her voice to a whisper and looking around to see that

Elisabeth Kapelian's Red Cross (Civil Defense) identification card.

no one was near, she informed me that the Gestapo wanted me for interrogation.

Panic gripped me as I realized the gravity of the situation. Madame la Directrice led me to a corner and made me sit down. She said, "The Germans probably want to send you to a work camp, but they might have learned about your other activities."

"Do you think they will punish my family?"

"Probably not." She was worried about me. Because the Germans had me under surveillance, it would be too dangerous for me to remain in Paris.

I didn't realize it at the time, but later I reasoned that Madame la Directrice was responsible for my involvement with the Resistance. She was well aware of my anti-German feelings and my independence. She had been impressed with my abilities as a Red Cross nurse and knew the Resistance desperately needed good nurses.

"I have to call Maman," I told Madame la Directrice.

"No," she replied. "It will be better if you do not; that way your Maman can answer honestly if the Gestapo asks her about you." Madame la Directrice assured me she would inform Maman later. "Plans are being made to get you out of Paris," she continued.

Although I felt terrified and confused, I followed her orders without question. I knew I must leave immediately.

A truck was already waiting.

All night we drove away from Paris, and the sun was well up over the horizon when the truck finally stopped, this time for good. Someone lifted the canvas covering and we all jumped out, tired and hungry. It felt good to stretch our cramped muscles.

After driving hours on back roads, we stopped at a very small village just a few miles from Auxerre. The area was wooded, hilly, and very beautiful. The truck driver escorted us to an old farmhouse hidden a short distance ahead. It reminded me of my grandparent's house, except it was run-down and much less attractive. We went immediately to the kitchen, where we were fed hard rolls and hot coffee. I warmed my hands by wrapping them around the coffee cup. We were all famished and ate hungrily in silence.

I tried to make conversation with the girl who had sat next to me on the truck. I found her just as unfriendly as she had been earlier. When I asked her where she came from, she whispered that we were not supposed to talk about personal information and looked away. When I reminded her that she knew I came from Paris, she glanced at me with her huge hazel eyes and said, "Be quiet! No more questions."

After breakfast, a boy with a limp summoned us through a side door, one by one. Finally, my turn came. I followed him into a large room where a stocky man sat at a table. He had swarthy skin and black snapping eyes which seemed to penetrate everything.

"Sit down, Mademoiselle," he said as he pointed to the only other chair in the room. "I see you are a nurse. That's very good, we need nurses very much." Then while shuffling through more papers, he asked me my name. When I started to tell him he interrupted me and said he did not want to know my real name. He wanted me to choose a name.

I thought a moment and answered, "Lisette."

"Good," he said, "your name from this time on shall be Lisette. You are a part of the the Resistance now. Put the past out of your mind." He paused while looking at me intensely with his penetrating eyes. Then in a very serious tone of voice, he said, "Don't confide in anyone your real name or what you are wanted for."

Next, he informed me that I would be assigned to their medical team, and from that moment on I should think of myself only as Lisette. "Now, Geoff will take you to your assignment."

Geoff, a tall, thin boy with pimples on his face and straggly red-blonde hair, grinned and said, "Lisette, I like that. It suits you." Geoff led me to a dilapidated car and drove me several miles to another farmhouse.

I walked into the main room of the farmhouse that served as an infirmary. On the floor, lay men and boys, all active members of the Resistance, either ill or wounded fighting the Germans. Some had blankets and pillows, but most were covered with jackets and rolled up clothing to pillow their heads. An unoccupied cot stood conspicuously in the corner.

"This is our treatment table," an older woman spoke as she walked up to me. She extended her hand and introduced herself as Marie. "If you are a nurse, you are more than welcome."

I introduced myself as Lisette and told her that I had worked as a civil defense nurse with the Red Cross. She seemed pleased and informed me, "You will be treating illnesses and diseases as well as injuries."

Evidently I appeared bewildered because Marie said I looked "dead on my feet" and ordered me to the back room for some badly needed sleep. She would show me my duties the next day.

I fell asleep immediately on a makeshift pallet on the floor. When I awoke, it was daylight. Marie was already working when I made my way to the infirmary. She spotted me immediately and began introducing me to patients and explaining their injuries and illnesses.

At the same time, the head physician, Dr. Soutille, walked up and introduced himself. He motioned me to follow him, commenting, "I am going to teach you how to treat venereal disease. This will be a part of your job," he explained as he led me to a *Maquisard* — Resistance fighter — who lay on the treatment cot. The *Maquisard* looked very pale and very young.

Dr. Soutille had the youth unbutton his pants and expose his penis. I looked away. "Lisette, pay attention," Dr. Soutille snapped at me. Dr. Soutille then inserted a catheter into the young man's penis, washed his bladder, and injected medication with a syringe. The boy's face contorted with pain and a moan escaped from his colorless lips.

"I cannot do this," I told Dr. Soutille.

"You have no choice," he replied. "You are here to help and you will do what needs to be done." His face softened as we walked away from the young soldier and he patiently explained to me what a horrible disease syphilis could be if left untreated. He admitted I would find this difficult to do at first, but I would get used to it. "Just remember that without treatment these young men could die."

We always treated the venereal disease patients on the cot in the corner of the room. Though I dreaded the duty, I became accustomed to it sooner than I expected.

One day a young man I had not seen before lay on the treatment cot. His eyes were closed when I approached him and I set about unbuttoning his pants. Some of the young men preferred to keep their eyes closed during treatment because of embarrassment or to prevent tears of pain. Suddenly, he grabbed my wrist in a vise-like grip as he sat up and said in a demanding voice, "What are you doing, little girl?"

Startled, I gasped and asked, "What?"

Just as suddenly, my "patient" burst into booming laughter. "I usually like to make my own advances," he said, "but you're so pretty that I might make an exception in this case." He had brown eyes, crisp dark curls, and a very infectious smile. I could not help but laugh along with him.

Marie came across the room. "He knows what you thought," she said. "He tries this on all the new nurses. This is Alex, our prankster. Alex, meet Lisette." Marie then turned to Alex and told him it looked like he had met his match this time.

"At least you didn't run and hide or cry like they usually do," Alex said as he smiled at me. "You really are a cool one and if I ever need a nurse, I'll choose you." Then he swaggered out the door and called back to me, "I'll see you soon, little girl."

I found myself smiling as I went about my work. The work was hard and frequently depressing, and it helped to laugh now and then. Occasionally, I was rewarded with a grateful smile or squeeze of my hand. Some were determined to flirt with me, but I learned early that it only complicated matters if I had patients vying for my attention. When I finished caring for them, I scrubbed the work area and washed soiled linen.

After about a week, our entire infirmary moved to an old hotel on the edge of Auxerre, provided by the owner, also a member of the Resistance. Few German troops were stationed in the Auxerre area, which made life a little more secure and pleasant for all of us. Packing and moving, I quickly learned, was a basic part of the lifestyle for everyone in the Resistance. Until after the Normandy invasion in June, we usually moved every few days, always within the Auxerre area. This made it more difficult for the Germans to determine our location. We moved in accordance with our instructions from London, where our sabotage missions were assigned. These instructions came over BBC — British Broadcasting Company — radio in code. Our officers, of course, handled these messages; I knew nothing of such matters at the time.

After the war, I read about how the Allies used the BBC to send codes to the French Resistance, alerting the *Maquis* to the timing of the landings in Normandy. I learned that the first and second line of Paul Verlaine's poem, "Chanson d'automne" — "Song of Autumn" — had been chosen as the code to inform the Resistance of the coming invasion. The first line, when broadcast, alerted the underground:

> *Les sanglots longs des violons de l'automne*
> The long sobs of the violins of autumn . . .

and the second line, when broadcast, indicated that the invasion would take place within 48 hours:

> *Blessent mon coeur d'une langueur Monotone*
> Wound my heart with a monotonous languor . . .[14]

As a nurse, I knew only when we were told it was time to pack up the infirmary supplies and move again. We traveled mostly in trucks, in wooded areas on the back roads, and always at night. Our trucks were old charcoal-burning vehicles scrounged from local farmers. They billowed black smoke as they inched down the roads.

While at Auxerre our unit received two more recruits. One was a fat, ugly doctor with a wooden leg, Captain Gautier. He was generally obnoxious, and I immediately disliked him. The other recruit was a nurse — the thin, blonde girl I had met on the truck.

The next day, from a distance, I observed the new girl working and was surprised to see how competent she was. I watched her for awhile and when she took a break, I extended my hand and said *"Bonjour."* I introduced myself as Lisette and told her we would be working together.

She looked at me and smiled shyly while wiping her hands on her skirt.

"*Bonjour*," she replied as she pumped my hand enthusiastically. "I'm Michelle," she responded, after which she apologized for being rude when we met on the truck.

"You were right." I told her, "I just hadn't known it at the time."

Stretcher bearers brought in several casualties and Michelle and I went back to work, cleaning wounds and changing bandages. One young man with a severe head injury started convulsing as I worked on him. I inserted a rag in his mouth, as I had done often when Annick had her seizures. Captain Gautier limped over to see if he could help. I was putting pressure on the gaping head wound to control the bleeding when he said harshly, "There is nothing you can do for him. Go work on someone you can help."

I ignored him and continued my ministrations. The young man's breathing became labored and finally stopped. Tearfully, I went to the next patient. This was the first time that a patient had died while in my direct care.

Captain Gautier looked up approvingly as I worked on a young *Maquisard* with a wounded arm. The bullet had gone all the way through his upper arm just missing bone and major blood vessels. But he had lost a lot of blood and felt dizzy. I bandaged his arm and had him hold his head between his knees so that he would not pass out.

"Nurse, I need you over here," Captain Gautier yelled to me. I looked around and saw I was the only one available. A *Maquisard* moaned in pain from a broken leg. The bullet had entered his upper thigh, fractured the leg, and lodged deep in the muscle. "You must hold him while I dislodge the bullet," Captain Gautier explained.

The boy shook as I put my arms around him to keep him still. I could sense his fear and whispered to him that he would be fine.

Captain Gautier probed for the bullet with forceps. It seemed to me that he was very rough and uncaring. The boy whimpered and cried out. A clink in the metal basin told me the bullet had been extracted. "Hold him tight, I must set his leg," Captain Gautier advised me. The boy screamed and passed out.

While I was helping to put the splint in place, Captain Gautier brushed against my breast, then flashed a lewd grin. I cringed and decided to keep my distance from the ugly, fat, slimy creature.

We worked hard the next few hours. Finally, all the wounded were cared for and I began cleaning up, making the patients as comfortable as possible. Captain Gautier approached me and placed his pudgy hand over mine. I pulled away, not even trying to suppress the revulsion I felt. "Keep your hands to yourself," I said before walking away in disgust.

Michelle gave her last medication and walked over to me. "I am glad that's over," she said. The front of her dress was soaked with blood and she had a smear across her left cheek. "So much blood," she said. "I'm covered with it and I'm just too tired to care."

Marie walked over and advised us to get some rest while we could. She also complimented us for the excellent job we had done, and told us that unless there was an emergency, in the future we would work in shifts.

The second story of the hotel had been set aside for the medical personnel so we all had our own room, an unaccustomed luxury for members of the Resistance. Michelle's room and mine adjoined, so we walked up together. Although friendships were discouraged, our age and circumstances encouraged bonding, and we worked well together. Michelle was sometimes timid and pessimistic, but she had a quick mind and a good sense of humor. It seemed natural for us to form an attachment.

I avoided Captain Gautier whenever possible, without being too obvious about it. He brushed against me at every opportunity, and he called me "darling" and "little cat." I didn't even think he was a good medic, because he treated his patients roughly and ignored good personal hygiene habits. Michelle noticed he liked being around me and commented on it. I only replied, "He is a fat, slimy pig."

I worked hard and went to my room to rest whenever time permitted. One day I had just arrived at my room when I saw Captain Gautier approaching, carrying two glasses in one hand and a bottle of champagne in the other. A wicked grin crossed his face. I hurried to my room, but in my haste, dropped my key. I unlocked the door as fast as I could, but before I could close and lock it, he forced his way into my room.

"Get out of my room this instant!" I yelled at him.

"Alright," he said soothingly, "but first have a drink with me." He calmly set the bottle and glasses on the table by the bed and then locked the door.

I ran to the door but he blocked me. "I am going to scream," I warned.

He grabbed me, threw me on the bed, and clamped his hand over my mouth. "You are so pretty, I just want to hold you," he coaxed.

His breath reeked of alcohol and I wanted to vomit. I bit his hand and he jerked away, grinning as I fought him. I hammered his body with my fists as I struggled to get away, but he had me pinned down. I managed to clip him on the jaw with my elbow and that distracted him enough for me to get out from beneath him and slip away. I scrambled over the end of the bed. He tried to follow me, but his wooden leg got wedged in the metal footboard of the bed and he fell. With a large crack, the wood splintered and he screamed. I glanced at him to see what had happened, picked up the wooden peg, and hit him over the head with it. He sank to the floor in a daze and I ran screaming out of the room.

I ran downstairs to the infirmary where I explained to Marie what happened. She quickly summoned the guards. I was still sobbing as they took him away. "Please, little cat. I'm sorry. Forgive me," he pleaded with me as they walked him out. Then he turned to the guards and said, "It was just a lovers' quarrel."

When Michelle came into my room that evening, I told her what had happened. She informed me that he had been telling everyone that we had been lovers for some time. "Of course, I did not believe him, but I'm afraid for your sake that there are those who do," she said.

I tried to ignore the episode, but Marie was especially cool to me the next day. Two of the boys who helped out in the infirmary made rude and suggestive comments to me. Even Michelle seemed to shun me. *She is probably afraid my bad reputation will rub off on her*, I thought.

I felt lonely and sad and kept to myself as much as possible. But I finally became so angry about the situation that I decided to take action. I approached Dr. Soutille, the head physician. He had always been kind and treated his patients with consideration. He was handsome in a fatherly sort of way and happily married. His wife and two children lived near Metz and he never missed the opportunity to show their pictures to anyone who expressed interest.

I told Dr. Soutille that I needed to talk to him and asked if I could meet him in private. He agreed without hesitating, and told me to meet him in the bandage room in 15 minutes. I was waiting when Dr. Soutille came into the room. It contained two hard chairs on which we sat while preparing bandages. He closed and locked the door and then asked me to sit down and tell him what I needed to discuss.

My eyes misted when I saw the sympathetic look on his face. I wiped them hurriedly, hoping he would not notice, and told him about the rumors Captain Gautier had been spreading about me. Dr. Soutille replied he was aware of what he had been saying.

I assured him that it was not true. "I am not his lover. I have never been anyone's lover." I hung my head and began to cry.

He said he believed me as he patted me on the shoulder. "What can I do to help?"

I told him, "Everyone is talking about me. They think I am a bad girl. I want you to examine me to prove that I am still a virgin."

He replied that he did not think it was necessary to go that far. I told him I thought it was the only way to prove that Captain Gautier was lying about me.

Just then, someone tried to get into the room, finally knocking after finding the door locked. Dr. Soutille opened the door and Marie charged in, demanding to know what was going on. Then turning to me, she spat, "Are you after this man too, you little tramp?"

Dr. Soutille stepped between Marie and me. "You owe this girl an apology, Marie. She came to me because Captain Gautier's false accusations have turned her colleagues against her. I felt she was exaggerating the situation until you accused her. My examination proves she is still a virgin and that Captain Gautier has lied. I expect you to inform her co-workers about this. I will deal with Gautier myself."

Marie's face flamed with embarrassment, but she turned to me and apologized. "You are a good worker and I'm relieved to know the truth. I shall see to it that everyone shares this information," she told me.

I smiled for the first time in days and felt grateful to Dr. Soutille for coming to my defense. To this day I have a special place in my heart for this gentle and wonderful man.

The incident with Captain Gautier was very humiliating, and I shall never forget it. I would not like to leave the impression that such degrading treatment of women was common in the Resistance. Quite the opposite was true; we were treated — at least in my unit — with both respect and fairness by the men.

There were approximately 150 resistants in my company, although the number varied from time to time and we were normally scattered in various locations in much smaller units. On the average, about nine or ten were women. Most were nurses, like me, although a few worked in the communications sections. Only one woman in four in the organized Resistance survived the war.

Except for my experience with Dr. Gautier, I don't think any of us had a serious problem involving what today would be called "sexual harassment." Most of the men were very protective of the women, especially the young girls, and treated us like "little sisters" or like their own daughters. Sometimes the younger men, like Alex, teased and called us "baby," "sexy," or something similar. But, we were not offended, because we trusted them. We knew they were just having fun, so in truth, we enjoyed their little games.

Now, when I stop and think about the low status of women in France at that time, the respect we received from the men was nothing less than remarkable. French women could not even vote until after the war! Nurses could serve in the French army but held no rank. Later, when our unit was incorporated into the First French Army, I became a victim of this absurd policy.

We suffered no such discrimination in the Resistance. As *Maquisards,* we were totally committed to driving the hated Germans from our country. To accomplish this goal, we developed strong feelings for one another. Men or women, we were comrades, united in our cause, and we paid little attention to our differences. Job performance was the only criteria on which we were judged.

When I reflected on all that had happened since leaving Paris, I felt very good about my achievements. I had accomplished my goal of joining the Resistance and serving my country. I was an active member of the *Maquis de l'Etang-Neuf (Yonne)* unit which I later learned was a part of the *Reseau Jean-Marie* Resistance group.[15] I was distressed about the many casualties I had treated because more and more were coming in each day. I was happy to do my duty, but wished more French men and women would join the Resistance so that we could end the war more quickly.

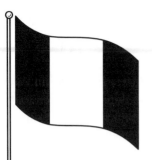

... General Charles de Gaulle, ... told us the "supreme battle," the battle for France, had begun. All "sons of France" had the "simple and sacred duty ... to fight the enemy by every means in their power."

Chapter 7

FOLLOWING MY TALK WITH Dr. Soutille, and then Marie, everyone greeted me at work the next morning with smiles, and the ugly incident with Gautier seemed forgotten. Best of all, Captain Gautier stayed away from me. Marie assigned me to work with Dr. Soutille, who told me that Captain Gautier had asked for a transfer and would be leaving soon.

A few days later while I was organizing supplies, Alex rushed into the infirmary and grabbed me by the hand. "Come with me," he said, while picking up a first aid kit as I ran out the door. "We just saw an American plane go down in the forest. We must beat the Germans to it."

I ran after Alex as he rushed through the field and into the woods. It had rained the night before and it was so hot I could almost see steam rising from the standing water. As we entered the forest, I had to push branches aside to make a path. I saw smoke rising through the dense trees just a few meters away. I prayed we could save the pilot as we drew near the crash.

Suddenly, the plane exploded and I could see a ball of fire ascending through the trees. "Damn," Alex cursed as he sprinted the last several meters. Struggling to keep up, I lost sight of him. The plane had crashed in a thicket of trees and bits of debris burned everywhere. I could feel the intense heat on my face as the plane blazed fiercely. I protected my eyes with my forearm and inched closer to the plane. The cockpit canopy stood open and a body lay sprawled nearby.

The young pilot was unconscious when I reached him. Alex pulled him away from the burning plane so he would be safe in case there was another explosion. He handed me the first aid kit and began to search the area for other survivors.

I knelt beside the injured man. He was alive, but just barely. Both legs were broken and he bled profusely from a deep cut just above his right eye. I checked his pupils and they were unequal, indicating possible brain injury. I applied a pressure bandage to his head wound and straightened out his broken legs. He began to groan, and I attempted to reassure him by softly stroking his hand.

Finally, the injured pilot opened his eyes, stared straight at me, and said something unintelligible. I knew he saw someone else, not me. Unable to find other survivors, Alex returned and asked me how the pilot was doing.

"I think very badly," I replied, while checking the bleeding from his head wound. It seemed to be slowing, but that could be bad news if he was bleeding internally and if his blood pressure dropped.

A short time later, a stretcher crew arrived and took the injured pilot to the infirmary. Dr. Soutille shook his head as he examined him; his chest was crushed and he began having trouble breathing. His name tags indicated he was Thomas O'Malley. He had curly red hair, freckles, and deep green eyes. I thought he would be very handsome under different circumstances.

Dr. Soutille continued to do what he could. His right leg was crushed and would need to be amputated if he lived, but he was too badly injured to withstand surgery at the time. Dr. Soutille turned to me and said, "We will have to wait and see, Lisette. I doubt that he will survive the night."

I stayed with the pilot, and my voice and touch seemed to calm him. *Poor Thomas, so far from home.* I wondered if he had a wife or a sweetheart in America.

He opened his eyes every now and then and looked at me. I continued speaking softly to him and smiling. I wanted him to know that I cared. Once he smiled and tried to say something that I could not understand. I thought it might have been a girl's name. Then he reached out and tried to touch my face, but he was too weak.

I bathed his face and stroked and held his hand. Around midnight, his breathing became labored and he lapsed into a deep coma. Finally, at about 3 o'clock in the morning, he died. By that time I had watched many men die, but there was something about the death of Thomas that nearly broke my heart. I cried like a baby as I removed his name tags. I felt responsible. All my life I had wanted to become a nurse to help people and save lives. Now I had achieved my goal but I could do nothing more than sit by his bed, hold his hand, and watch him die.

War is so stupid and senseless, I thought. *If Thomas had lived, who knows what great things he may have accomplished?* At the very least, the gentle look on his face told me he certainly would have been a wonderful husband and father. But he was dead, and the world would never know what he might have done or become. And none of us, not even Dr. Soutille, could do anything but watch. I don't think I had ever felt more helpless. It was a very sad experience, and it made a deep impression on me. Even now, I have a vivid recollection of that terrible night when I held the hand of my dying American pilot, Thomas O'Malley, a man I never knew.

On June 6, 1944, the long awaited Allied invasion finally took place on the shores of Normandy. We received the exciting news on the same day, while working in the infirmary. Very briefly, all work ceased while we rejoiced. We kissed everyone while crying with joy. We knew the war was nearing its end and France would soon be free again. Also, we held a moment of silence while each of us prayed in our own way that peace would come quickly. I think we all felt a tremendous sense of pride, knowing that *Maquis* units all over France had played in important part in setting the stage for the historic invasion. As nurses, we were not personally involved in blowing up bridges and trains, but we tended to the wounds of the brave *Maquisards* who had carried out the sabotage missions. That was enough for me. Whenever the thought occurred to me that I played even a small role in making D-Day a success, my heart pounded and I beamed with pride and fulfillment.

On the same day the Allies landed at Normandy, our Battalion Commander, Colonel Jacques Adam, called an assembly of our entire unit to tell us what we should expect in the coming weeks. "While the Allied armies would advance," he said, "the worst fighting is yet to come. The Germans can be expected to surrender French territory only after the most stubborn resistance. All Frenchmen must fight courageously until the enemy has been completely driven from French soil."

That same evening we all gathered around a radio and listened to an address by General Charles de Gaulle, who had become the symbol of the French Resistance. Speaking on the BBC to the French people, he told us the "supreme battle," the battle for France, had begun. All "sons of France" had the "simple and sacred duty . . . to fight the enemy by every means in their power."[16] The words were inspiring, and at the moment everyone seemed happy. However, we realized, there were many difficult days to come. Even before the invasion, we had seen an increase in our casualties due to the intensification of sabotage activity in preparation for the invasion. Now, with Allied forces and *Maquisards* both openly engaged in fighting the Germans, we could expect to see even higher casualties.

After the Normandy invasion, everyone wanted to become a part of the Resistance, and our numbers increased accordingly. *Where were all of these sunshine patriots before the Allies landed, when we really needed help? If they had joined earlier, perhaps France would already be free.*

It was exciting to see so many volunteers for the Resistance, but it became difficult to feed everyone. Additional Allied airdrops helped, but did not satisfy our needs. Normally, we received most of our food from local farmers who supported the Resistance. They gave us food, especially fruit in the orchards, which we could pick for ourselves. On occasion, some of our men worked on farms in exchange for food. Sometimes the men shot or trapped wild game, such as rabbits or pheasants, which we considered a rare treat. Local restaurant owners sympathetic to the Resistance supplied us with coffee — though of poor quality. We routinely ate bread and cheese and drank wine, probably because they were cheaper than most other items. Whatever the source, we managed to obtain adequate quantities of food, but the huge increase in our numbers made the task more difficult.

One day, not long after the invasion, I found myself with some rare free time on my hands. I learned from Charles, one of the older *Maquisards*, that he and several others planned to blow up the tracks for a train scheduled to pass nearby on its way to Germany. Presumably the train would pick up supplies and deliver French workers to help in German factories.

I had long been curious about the acts of the saboteurs. This mission, to plant explosives on railroad tracks seemed custom-ordered for me. Nervously, I went to Charles and asked him to please let me go along with them, carefully assuring him that I would not get in the way.

"Absolutely not," he answered. "We cannot be responsible for your safety and you are needed too much here."

I let the subject drop, but I knew the time and place of their departure. Just before they left, I found a beret to cover my black curly hair, put on a brown shirt, and slipped on some black trousers several sizes too large for me. My heart pounded with excitement as I walked to the departure point. Charles was already briefing his group, all young men dressed in dark clothing. I stayed in the background, hoping no one would notice me, but Charles looked up when I arrived. He grimaced when he saw me, but continued on with his instructions. When he finished and answered all the questions, he walked over and told me I was a very stubborn girl. I smiled.

Charles agreed to let me come, but said I must stay under cover at all times and watch from a safe distance. I assured him I would follow all orders and gave him a smart salute, a gesture that almost caused my large pants to come down. He laughed, handed me a piece of rope, and told me to use it as a belt to keep them up. I threaded it through the belt loops and knotted it tightly.

I felt the excitement building as I followed the team through a forest located east of Auxerre. I felt alive and happy to be hiking through the trees, away from the infirmary and the sick and injured. We hiked for approximately two hours before reaching the tracks. The sun was going down as they prepared the explosives. Charles motioned for me to get back, so I retreated to the edge of the woods and watched from a distance. Before they were finished, I heard a train whistle. As the train approached — I could see the smoke from the engine — our men were still setting the explosives. I was afraid they would not finish in time, but they completed the job quickly and retreated to the cover of the forest.

The train was in sight when the track blew up. The engine and several cars went off the track and overturned. I heard the screams of women and children from a derailed boxcar. Frightened people, packed in like sardines, scrambled over each other trying to escape.

Some of the people ran toward me as German soldiers carrying machine guns appeared from the train, yelling at them. Charles stopped short and fired at the Germans with his rifle in an effort to divert them from the terrified prisoners. Several other *Maquisards* beckoned to the escapees, encouraging them to run toward the forest. Many of the prisoners were Jews — men, women, and children — all displaying the yellow Star of David on their coat lapels.

The Germans opened fire. They shot the fleeing prisoners in the back as they were trying to escape, but some made it to safety. A bullet hit Charles in the arm and Louis was killed outright — shot in the head. Charles motioned for me to follow as he dragged Andre, one of his men, into the forest. Charles threw Andre over his shoulder and carried him until he was sure the German soldiers were no longer following. When he finally dropped to the ground, I was right beside him. Andre was dead. As Charles lay there, trying to catch his breath, I checked his arm.

"I'm all right," Charles said. "See about the others."

Ignoring him, I ripped his shirt sleeve off and bound his arm. "You're bleeding," I countered. "If I don't get the bleeding stopped, you won't be any good to anyone." I told Charles he was brave but foolhardy, and he should get some rest while I looked after the others.

Pierre was uninjured, but two men were killed, and one wounded — a heavy price to pay, but the mission had been accomplished. A number of those who had escaped from the train were taken back to Auxerre where a member of the underground took them into hiding.

I could not stop thinking about the fleeing prisoners and my dead companions, and depression threatened to overtake me. Louis, a jovial young man only 18 years old, had frequently helped in the infirmary. He planned to be a doctor. *This damned war, taking so many lives. How could the survivors ever be the same? And what about the Jewish prisoners on the train; where were the Germans taking them?* We had heard terrible stories, but we had no certain information about their fate.

I worked very hard during the next several days, which kept me from dwelling on the vision of fleeing women and children shot in the back by the Germans. Charles dropped into the infirmary frequently to get his wound checked and the bandage changed. He also came by just to visit and we became good friends. Charles was a stocky man in his early twenties with dark receding hair. He enjoyed talking to me and kidding me about my boldness, sense of adventure, and energy, while I enjoyed stories of his numerous missions for the underground.

During these days, I was very proud to be a member of the Resistance and to uphold the honor of the French people. I eagerly looked forward to the day when France would be liberated. The Allies had invaded and volunteers continued joining the Resistance in record numbers. *Surely, the end of German oppression cannot be far off.*

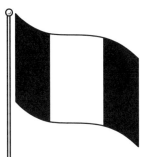

*. . . When the **Milice** returned, they shouted obscenities and angrily began beating and kicking me until I again lapsed into unconsciousness. I remember two of the **Milice** taking me away from the prison . . . to the Gestapo.*

Chapter 8

ONE DAY, approximately two and a half months after the invasion of Normandy, while we were still in the vicinity of Auxerre, Charles told me he was going on a mission. He asked if I would like to go along and act as their lookout. Always ready for a new adventure, I accepted without hesitation. We left at dawn the next morning. Our objective: to destroy a German munitions train. Charles gave me a small pistol to take along.

Charles, three others, and I hiked several miles to the point where we would plant the explosives. They positioned me in the woods approximately 75 yards from the track. Charles and his men were working on the tracks when I heard dogs barking in the distance. I ran to Charles and informed him that they must hurry because German patrols were near. He looked up impatiently and told me to "get out of sight"; they were almost finished.

They continued working while the barking grew louder and louder. *Something must have gone wrong*, I thought, and I left my protective cover to check on their progress. *Perhaps, I can help.* I walked into the clearing just as the Germans appeared. They pointed their guns straight at us. There was no escape.

I shivered with fright as I looked into the arrogant faces of my captors. Their leader motioned for us to kneel on the ground with our hands in the air. He circled us, roughly forcing our hands behind our backs and tying them with ropes. I was certain I was going to die, and when I looked at Charles, I knew he felt the same way. He looked at me and whispered that he was sorry. I managed a small smile at him to let him know that I did not blame him for our fate.

A shot rang out and we all fell to the ground. I was surprised when I did not feel any pain; the bullet had not hit me. Then I heard voices, looked around, and saw that everyone was okay except Charles, who lay motionless with a bloody, gaping wound in the back of his head. I gasped as fear gripped me. I knew they were going to kill all of us, one at a time. *What could be more cruel than seeing your companions die one by one, always wondering who would be next?*

Shots rang out, one at a time. I heard the shot meant for me, but I didn't feel the bullet.

One of the Germans stood over me and laughed. I tried to stand up, but had trouble getting my balance because my hands were tied behind my back. I managed to get half-way up on my knees when he kicked me in the back with his boot, and I fell to the ground. The blows kept coming as he continued to kick me in the stomach while yelling obscenities. *Death*, I thought, *could not be far away*. Then blackness descended and I lost consciousness.

When I awoke, I found myself in a tiny cell with no furnishings or windows, just walls and a wooden floor. I heard people moaning and crying, but I had no idea where I was. I only knew I was in custody. I did not realize until I turned over and felt pain in my groin that I still carried the small pistol Charles had given me. It had dropped into my underwear and was lodged in my panties. I lay there in pain the rest of the day and night without food or water, never doubting I was going to die.

The next day, a young Frenchman entered my cell. Strong and stocky with blond hair and blue eyes, he looked German, but he wore the black beret, black boots, and uniform of the French *Milice*. My heart sank; I would have preferred to remain in the custody of the Germans. Like most of the French, I hated and feared the mercenary *Milice* more than the Germans.

The young Frenchman pulled me to my feet and asked me my name. "What have we here, a baby?" he asked.

I said nothing.

He gripped my arm tightly and said, "I asked you a question, bitch."

I spit in his face.

He doubled his fist, hit me squarely on my jaw and I fell to my knees. Next, he kicked me, forced me back on my feet, and took me into the hall where I viewed several other prisoners locked in a larger cell, their eyes staring blankly and some moaning in pain. They looked so hurt, so pitiful, lying on the floor in their own excrement that I turned my head away.

He forced me to look. "This is what happens to proud resistants," he said, "when they refuse to talk." He took me back to my cell and threw me inside, warning me to think about what I had just seen.

When he left, I thought about all the horrors — the death, disease, maimed and burned bodies — I had observed in the past few months since joining the Resistance and of all the brave prisoners I had just seen. *How they had suffered at the hands of the traitorous* Milice. *Could I do it? Could I be that brave?* I prayed to God to give me the strength to endure what I must without betraying my people.

Miraculously, I drifted into a half sleep. I began dreaming and saw the face of Papa. His quiet, gentle smile looked at me with such pride. I heard his laughter, and felt myself enfolded in his arms making me feel loved and cherished. I awoke with a start; Papa wasn't there. He was dead, killed by the same enemy, the Germans. *I will die too*, I thought. But Papa will greet me in heaven. That seemed to give me some comfort and I slept again.

I woke up the next morning so sore that I could hardly move. My insides were so painful and I was bleeding from cuts from the top to the bottom of my body. I was removed from my cell for further questioning.

Three of the *Milice* grabbed me and ripped off my blouse and bra, leaving me naked from the waist up. They put me on the floor and held me. *My God*, I thought, *they are going to rape me!* As one of them hovered over me, fear turned to anger, I reached into my panties, grabbed the pistol and fired at him right through my panties. I must have hit him because others immediately came to his aid and helped him out of the room.

When the *Milice* returned, they shouted obscenities and angrily began beating and kicking me until I again lapsed into unconsciousness. I remember two of the *Milice* taking me away from the prison in a big black car. When the *Milice* were unsuccessful in breaking a prisoner, they sent him or her to the Gestapo.

When I woke up the next morning, I was in a different cell. A large, fat German with a cruel smile came in and told me in a very thick French accent: "I am very sorry about the rough treatment by your own people. You are now in Gestapo custody and will be treated much better." He gave me a bowl of warm soup and told me: "If you are a good girl and tell me the name of your leader, I will let you go."

I refused to answer and he became very angry. He knocked me down and began kicking me. Then he completely destroyed my dignity by ripping off my clothes and making me walk around the building, a special prison for interrogation, completely naked. I was taken back to my cell where I vomited and lapsed into unconsciousness again. I didn't care whether I lived or died.

The next day, two large men picked me up in my cell and I took me to a large cold room. Inside were two bathtubs, one on each side of the room, and a big rectangular table with many surgical instruments. The bathtubs were filled with water and two of the pigs were standing nearby as though waiting for something. As I walked through the room, one of them asked if the bathtubs were for me.

The fat man who had questioned me before replied, "No." Then he turned to me, "You are much too young and too pretty to die. If you will only tell me the name of your unit and leader, you can go free."

I was no longer humiliated; I was angry. *I am a nurse!* They had no right to beat me for information. But the pigs didn't care. I looked into his face and yelled: "Only a stupid vermin would believe I knew anything of value to him!"

I could see his face becoming very red as he angrily told me they were going to give me shock treatment, then burn my eyes out, and if that did not work, break my fingers one by one after tearing out my fingernails. He ordered the men to place me on the table. I pretended to lapse into unconsciousness again as they began shocking me with electric wires. I passed out and awakened only after I felt a painful burning sensation. I looked down and saw two men burning my lower torso and legs with cigarette butts. I fainted again and woke up in my cell.

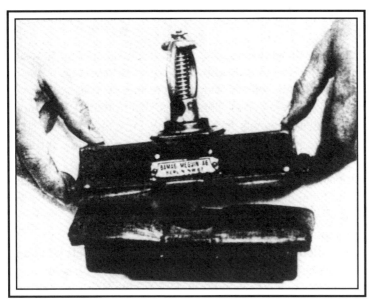

A thumb screw like that used by the Gestapo to torture Elisabeth Kapelian. To this day she carries the results on her left thumb, which had caused intolerable pain. She also lost the use of one kidney due to the beatings received.

The next day is only a blur in my memory. I remember only a series of sessions with different questioners, always ending with a beating, after which they dragged me back to my cell. Mostly they wanted to know the names of the Resistance leaders, especially my commander, and the location of units.

After enduring great pain at the hands of the Gestapo, I would either pretend to pass out, or I really would faint. But during the respite between beatings, my strength and anger returned. In those brief moments of recovery, my family life before the war, the German atrocities I'd witnessed, and my comrades in the Resistance all entered my mind. I remembered Papa saying good-bye to me at the train station, Victor and Denise torn from their home and baby in the middle of the night, my little sister lying in a hospital bed, little Marie going without milk, Charles face down in his own blood, Thomas O'Malley dying while I held his hand, Maman's depression, and the mother and baby shot in the subway. From those images and many more, I drew a will to fight back — to continue fighting for France. *God has a purpose for my fate!* I believed.

I told them absolutely nothing, not even the name of Colonel Adam. I knew that if you supplied information to the brutal Germans, you were no longer useful, and often killed immediately. The Resistance had intentionally kept us as uninformed as possible about important matters so that we could reveal nothing of value to the enemy, even if we were captured and tortured. We could not tell what we did not know.

Now, as I reflect on those difficult and painful days, I believe the self-discipline learned in the Catholic boarding schools, the hatred I felt for the Germans and the traitorous *Milice*, and my determination to see France liberated contributed to my survival. The values, determination, and motivation created by previous events in my life, plus my own natural stubbornness, gave me the will to live regardless of the torture they inflicted on me.

On the fifth morning of my captivity, I awoke to total silence. I remembered dreaming in the night of someone yelling from far away, "*Sauve qui peut*" — *Save yourself*. But, like the vision of my father's face, the voice could have been another trauma-induced illusion.

How strange the silence felt. Although I was kept in complete isolation, I could usually hear sounds of pain. There was no groaning, no screaming. *Where was everyone?* I looked around, noticing for the first time that my cell door stood open. I struggled to my feet only to find myself too weak to stand alone. I moved along the wall and stumbled out of the cell. There was no one in the hall. *Could I just walk out?*

Hope surged through me, giving me strength. I staggered out of the building into the sunlight. My cell had been dark and my face so damaged by beatings that the light hurt my eyes and I put my hand up to shield them. I saw someone coming towards me. I thought he was *Milice* or German and I turned to run. I knew that I didn't have long to live, as I obviously knew nothing and would tell nothing that could help the enemy. However, pain and weakness overcame me and I fainted.

I woke up in a small French hospital somewhere southeast of Auxerre. A man in a white uniform stood over my bed and he asked me how I was doing. I shrunk back on my pillows, terrified, replying that I did not know anything.

I felt a reassuring hand on my arm. "You are safe here, no one will hurt you," he said.

I was not convinced. "What happened?" I asked.

He replied that I had been liberated and brought to the hospital for treatment.

At first, I thought the man's explanation was only a trick to obtain information from me. My life had changed so dramatically in the past few days that I felt frightened and suspicious of everyone and everything.

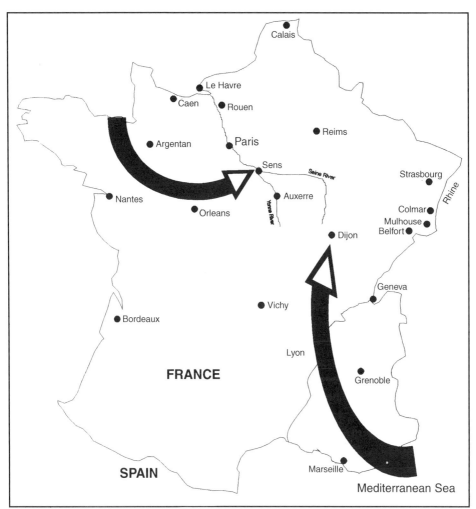

France, August-September 1944. The arrows show the routes of the advancing Allied troops. In early August, General Patton began his celebrated dash across northern France from Brittany to the Seine. On August 21st, units of Patton's Third Army liberated Sens. On August 15th, Allied forces landed on the coast of southern France and began their drive up the Rhône River. On September 11th, they reached Dijon, a city southeast of Auxerre, which the Germans had vacated. Realizing the danger of entrapment when the Allied armies from the north and south came together, the Germans began the mass evacuation of the approximately 100,000 troops stationed in southwestern France during the second half of August. The Auxerre area, where Elisabeth was imprisoned, would have been in the midst of these evacuations.[17,18] As a consequence she says, "It can be reasonably concluded that I was found and taken to the hospital by local citizens, or perhaps, by *Maquisards*, who pursued the fleeing Germans closely and harassed them at every possible opportunity."

Would I ever feel safe again? The days went by slowly, and with gentle care and good food, I found myself relaxing. I gradually grew stronger, and after eight days in the hospital, the doctors finally told me I could leave.

However, I had no place to go because I no longer knew the location of my unit. I had no money and no identification. I settled for a temporary shelter for refugees set up by the Allies, where I was provided with food and a cot.

After a few days, I began to face what had happened during the past two weeks. *God must have a reason for my survival.* I had difficulty comprehending the miracle of my rescue, but I knew I had been incredibly lucky. Still, I felt very vulnerable and alone. I was now free to go home, to Maman and Suzanne, but it never crossed my mind. My only thoughts were to find my fellow *Maquisards*, my new family, and return to complete the mission of liberating France.

I sat on the curb with my head down, trying to work out a plan. But I couldn't concentrate. Then I heard a young man near me ask, "Lisette? Lisette, is it really you?" I looked at the tall skinny man who stood before me. He looked vaguely familiar, but my traumatized mind could not remember who he was. Suddenly, I felt a surge of fear and I struggled to my feet and ran.

He followed me and grabbed my hand. I shrieked with pain. He had grabbed the same hand the Germans had injured so severely with the thumb screw. "Don't you remember me, Lisette?" he asked. "I'm Jean. We worked together in the Resistance; now I'm a photographer and journalist."

I began to smile as my mind finally made the connection. I did remember him. He went on to tell me how the *Maquis* thought I had been killed when I failed to return. When they discovered the bodies of Charles and three others, they assumed the Germans had shot me as well.

"I'm lucky to be alive," I said. But I did not want to discuss my incarceration, so I quickly changed the subject. I asked him what he was doing at the refugee camp.

He replied that his family lived nearby and he was home on leave.

"Jean," I pleaded, "I want to go back to my unit."

He looked at me with concern in his eyes. He asked me to come home with him, saying his parents would be honored to have me. He put his hand on mine and told me that I really looked like I needed a few days rest.

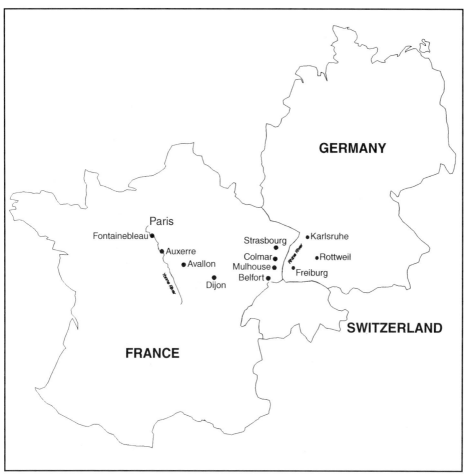

Elisabeth's locations with the *Maquis de l'Etang-Neuf (Yonne)* and later with the First French Army. Her Resistance unit was stationed in the Auxerre area, where she was imprisoned by the Gestapo. After she was liberated, she caught up with her unit at Avallon. A short time later, they moved toward Dijon, where they discovered their comrades buried alive.

Elisabeth attended boot camp near Belfort and was with the French army, stationed at Colmar, when her ambulance was hit by mortar and Michelle was killed; she was then transferred to Karlsruhe. After the war was declared over, Charlotte, Lucette, and Elisabeth celebrated in Strasbourg. They were later transferred to Freiburg and then to Rottweil in the Black Forest.

I told him what I really needed was work. "I need to keep busy. It is not good for me to sit around and think about myself."

He agreed to take me, but said I would have to ride with him on his bicycle, his only form of transportation. I smiled and assured him that the bike would be fine. For the first time in days, I felt hope again. *Maybe working will mend my mind and body and keep me from thinking about myself and what had happened to me.*

My unit had moved since my capture. The infirmary was now housed in a large barn near Avallon, about 50 kilometers southeast of Auxerre — four hours by bicycle. Upon arrival, I walked into the infirmary and went right to work as though I had never been away. When Michelle saw me, she threw her arms around me and sobbed. "What happened to you? I thought I would never see you again."

I skimmed over the recent events, told her I was doing fine, but needed to work so I could forget all about it. Michelle smiled and nodded that she understood. My friends and co-workers each came by and expressed their happiness that I had returned safely. I was grateful none of them asked questions about my captivity. They knew by my silence that I was not ready to talk about it.

I slept like a baby that night. I felt safe and protected, like I was at home. The next morning, Dr. Soutille summoned me to his office. "Lisette, we're happy to have you back with us. We had given up hope that you had survived."

I smiled, but said nothing. He asked me if I felt like telling him what had happened. I calmly told him about the mission and how we had been surprised by the German patrol while we were planting explosives on the tracks. I related how the Germans had killed Charles and then took me prisoner. But, I could not tell him about the horror of watching my comrades shot in cold blood, the attempted rape, the humiliation, the beatings, the electrocutions, the thumb screw, nor the cruel isolation I received while held captive; my mind just did not want to remember the cruelty. I told him they had hurt me, but nothing more.

Dr. Soutille patted me on my shoulder and asked, "Are you sure you are strong enough to go back to work, Lisette? Perhaps, you should take a few days off."

His remark frightened me because I knew I needed work — the more work the better. I looked at Dr. Soutille and pleaded, "Please, I need to work. It helps me to forget."

He smiled and said he understood; he too sometimes found life easier when very busy. He repeated how happy everyone was to have me back, and offered to listen if I ever felt the need to talk about my experiences.

I thanked him for his concern and understanding.

I spent the next few weeks trying to reconcile my feelings about what had happened, especially the guilt I felt for being the only survivor. *Why did Charles and the others die while I lived?* Perhaps the Germans believed that a woman would be easier to break, thus they captured me and killed the men, but I still felt guilty for surviving. I was deeply depressed. I relived the torture each night as I lay half-asleep. I believe my faith in God and the belief that He had future expectations of me helped me eventually accept the relentless physical pain imposed by the *Milice* and the German interrogators, and the psychological pain that continued to haunt me long after my liberation.

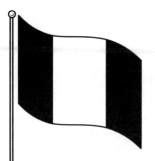

... In the clearing just ahead, human heads were scattered everywhere. . . . When we drew closer I realized the bodies were buried up to their necks.

Chapter 9

AFTER RETURNING FROM MY CAPTIVITY, I found we were busier than ever trying to take care of all the casualties. In August and September of 1944, the Allied armies were sweeping across France, liberating one city after another. This was the moment for which the *Maquis* units had been patiently waiting, and fighting between the *Maquisards* and the Germans increased sharply. Frequently the *Maquisards* played a major role in cleaning up pockets of Germans that had been bypassed by the Allied armies. My unit, the *Maquis de l'Etang-Neuf (Yonne)*, followed the First French Army led by General de Latter de Tassigny, who had invaded southern France in mid-August. Wherever they were, the *Maquisards* were busy fighting Germans, which of course, meant an increase in causalities and in our work at the infirmary.

We were ordered to move closer to Dijon, so we packed up and began our journey. Our convoy moved slowly through the forests, in the Department of Nievre, just west of Dijon. Suddenly the lead truck stopped. Word filtered to us that a German patrol had passed in front of us. We got out of our vehicles and waited for orders to proceed. When we started again, it was on foot with only the drivers in the vehicles. We could not take a chance on being ambushed by the Germans.

All *Maquisards* were told to hide in the forest during the night and to regroup in the morning. Michelle and I huddled together. Michelle whispered she thought we were going to be killed. Although I was frightened about being recaptured, I told her that the Boche were probably several kilometers away and we would be fine. We finally dozed off, but I awoke minutes later and could not go back to sleep.

Michelle continued to snore softly beside me, which pleased me. She sometimes annoyed me with her pessimistic outlook on life, always so suspicious of everyone and so certain that danger lurked around every corner, but I still loved her like a sister.

At dawn, we were awakened by Alex who told us it was time to move on. Led by Alex, our small party of seven proceeded by foot. We had walked about an hour when he stopped, put his fingers to his lips, and signaled everyone to stop. The woods were too quiet, too still. Not even the sound of birds chattering or wind rustling in the trees could be heard. It was total, frightening silence.

Alex moved forward with extreme caution while I followed close behind him. Suddenly he stopped, gasped, and tried to hold everyone back. I pushed past him and beheld a sight that would haunt my dreams for the rest of my life.

In the clearing just ahead, human heads were scattered everywhere. At first we thought they were separated from their bodies. However, when we drew closer I realized the bodies were buried up to their necks. I heard a groan and ran to the heads to determine if anyone was still alive. I checked them one by one, but they were all dead. There were about a dozen bodies. I kept hearing a groaning sound and suddenly realized the sounds were coming from my own throat.

By now, Michelle and her companions had joined us. Michelle screamed until Alex slapped her. Then she turned away and began to sob quietly. I spotted a boy in the ground about my age, perhaps a little older. Ants crawled over his sightless eyes. I started screaming and hysterically began brushing the ants away. Then I began digging furiously with my hands, trying to release this unknown boy from the earth. Alex grabbed me and pulled me away. I collapsed in helpless sobs as Alex held me. I could feel him crying too.

"We have to bury them properly!" I exclaimed. "We can't leave them like this for the insects and animals to feed upon."

Alex replied that we would bury them, but first we needed to return to the convoy for shovels.

"I will not leave them," I protested. "You take the others and I will stay with them until you return."

He could see that I meant what I said and did not argue. Jean, the same boy who had brought me back to the unit on his bicycle, was designated to stay with me. I felt sure those buried were *Maquisards*. *Why else would they have been slaughtered?*

The familiar hatred for the Germans and my anger toward them returned as I stood guard over the grisly graveyard. Yet, I forced myself to think of more pleasant things. I thought of my visits to Grandpere and Grandmere at their home in Villeneuve St. Georges, and the way Grandmere fussed around, preparing food, always making sure I had everything I needed. It was always good to be with them, to be cuddled and spoiled.

I loved the interchange between Grandmere and Grandpere. My Grandpere teased Grandmere constantly and never missed an opportunity to pat her on her behind and give her a little pinch. Then he would laugh and tell her how much he loved her and that he just could not keep his hands off her. Grandmere would often give her grandchildren gifts to take home, sometimes even gold coins or family jewels when we became old enough to appreciate them. I found myself smiling. I blessed my ability to escape into fond memories and thoughts when the world grew too painful for me — it was a special gift.

A short time later, a Colonel Poireau arrived and told us the dead were probably *Maquisards* from the Vercors, an isolated mountainous area south of Grenoble long recognized as a bastion of the Resistance. Colonel Poireau had brought a work party which promptly reburied the bodies. The brutal Germans or *Milice* had evidently tied the *Maquisards*' hands and feet together, tortured them, and then buried them. Most of the bodies had head wounds, indicating they were probably alive when they were buried. By then I was beyond crying. The horrors of the war had become too real, too personal.

But Michelle could not stop crying, a soft, helpless sobbing. With all the death she had seen, the scene was just too much for her to bear. I did the best I could to comfort her, but with no success. After a proper burial, Colonel Poireau held a small service in memory of our dead compatriots.

When we finished properly burying our fellow resistants, we moved on to our new post which was about 40 kilometers south of Dijon. We arrived at an abandoned farmhouse and Marie, Michelle, and I immediately began converting it into an infirmary. We used the first floor for the operating room, treatment areas, and recovery areas, and the second floor for patients. By working hard, we had the infirmary ready to treat patients by the end of the day.

On August 25, 1944, my beloved Paris was finally liberated, and on the following day General de Gaulle made his official entry into the city. Normally, the news of these exciting events would have been cause for joyous celebration at the infirmary. However, we were so busy taking care of the wounded we hardly noticed, let alone celebrated. I really do not remember the particular moment I first learned about these events, but as I recall, it was several days after they had taken place. At that time we were working long hours, sometimes as long as 18-hour shifts, and I did little else except work and sleep.

Michelle had hardly spoken since the discovery of our dead compatriots in the forest. She seemed to lose her appetite and developed a cough she was unable to shake. I advised her to report in sick and get some rest; we were expecting heavy casualties and would need her more later. She became indignant and told me in no uncertain terms that she was not a child and would make her own decisions, then softened her harsh reply with a smile.

One morning, Michelle woke up flushed and feverish with a rash all over her body. I took her to the infirmary and Dr. Soutille checked her over. He diagnosed her illness as measles complicated by pneumonia, and said she needed to be isolated. Marie overheard the conversation, and told us that we could take her to the farmhouse down the road. The old couple living there had been very generous with their food and supplies, and Marie was confident Michelle could stay with them. Marie even volunteered to take Michelle to them herself. When Marie returned a short time later, she reported that the couple were happy to help and Michelle was in excellent hands.

The next morning, casualties began arriving *en masse*. We were now treating French soldiers as well as *Maquisards*. Marie and I worked double shifts because we were short-handed. Marie helped in the operating room and I worked upstairs with the patients.

Alex was brought in with a chest wound, just barely conscious. He had been returning from a trip to pick up some food and supplies for the hospital. A German sniper had shot him while he was securing a loosened rope on the truck bed.

I panicked when I saw Alex. In spite of my efforts to remain detached from my patients, Alex became a special favorite of mine. We had shared so much together and I treasured our long friendship. I went to him and held his hand which was sticky with blood. He opened his eyes, looked at me and smiled. He tried to speak to me but started coughing blood. I said to him, "You are too young and too mean to die, and God doesn't want you anyway."

Fear gripped me as I took Alex into surgery, but the injury proved to be less serious than first thought. The bullet had broken a rib but fortunately missed his left lung. If the bullet had entered a few inches to the left or in his lower chest, he probably would have died. Although none of his major vessels were affected, he had lost a great deal of blood. Alex was very lucky to be alive.

But we had no time to agonize over one person when every cot and pallet in the infirmary was full. The retreating Germans still resisted stubbornly and inflicted heavy casualties on the advancing Allied forces. The number and severity of German atrocities had increased sharply. The Normandy landings had forced German units to move quickly, either to support German forces elsewhere or, to escape entrapment. In the process they were frequently harassed by the *Maquis*, and the enraged Germans had responded by carrying out brutal reprisals.

The *Tulle* executions that had been carried out earlier by the SS division, *Das Reich*, on June 9, 1944, are a good example of German retaliation. The Germans grabbed 99 men off the streets and hanged them, some by meat hooks. On the following day, the same SS division carried out the famous massacre at nearby Oradour-sur-Glane, where 642 men, women, and children died, most burned to death in a local church.

When the Germans smashed the Resistance stronghold in the Vercors on July 21, 1944, their reprisals included the slaughter of men, women, children, pets, and livestock, the mutilation of bodies, and the burning of entire villages.[19]

A couple of the young Resistance workers tried to help with our incoming wounded, but they were untrained and of limited usefulness. When Marie realized we could not possibly keep up, she requested help from the French army.

I stayed busy every moment, but made time to run by Alex's cot to check on him as often as possible. Alex was very sick after surgery. I watched him carefully until he was fully awake and complaining of pain, and then I knew he was alright.

I would work steadily for five days with only a few hours sleep caught at odd times. When I finally went to my room, I felt like a zombie. I would fall into bed fully clothed and sleep like a baby until Marie came to tell me that new casualties had arrived. Finally, when the new nurses and orderlies arrived from the army, I was able to sleep a full eight hours. I awoke fully refreshed, and had a nice cup of coffee before returning to the infirmary. Everyone seemed to be doing well and the morning routine was running smoothly. They were already transferring some patients to hospitals in nearby towns.

When I checked on Alex, he was laying on his side with his head down. He seemed to be asleep, but his breathing was rapid and uneven. I gave him a gentle touch and he jumped, waking up immediately. When I coaxed him to sit up, he looked as though he could not grasp what I was saying. His eyes were too bright and unfocused, and his face flushed. When I touched his forehead, he grabbed my hand and said, "Your hand is so cool, Anna." He was so hot and feverish, he could not even recognize me. He complained of being too warm and thirsty. I took his temperature and the thermometer read 104 degrees. I left for a few minutes to get some aspirin for his fever, and returned to find him quivering and shaking all over.

I summoned Dr. Soutille, who came immediately. He drained an abscess that had formed on Alex's chest wound and asked me to start an IV. I tried to give Alex an aspirin, but in his delirium, he kept pushing me away. I bathed his burning body with cool water and alcohol. Whenever I turned my back, he pulled the IV out of his arm. Finally, I got some aspirin down him, which he vomited up immediately. All evening, I sat by his cot, held his hand, and talked to keep him calm. Each time I took my hand away, he became agitated so I stayed with him. He was finally able to keep some aspirin in his stomach and he drifted into a restless sleep. The IV and the aspirin began to work and his fever broke. He entered a deep, natural, healing sleep just before daybreak.

"*Merci, Mon Dieu!*" — *Thank you, God* — I shouted when I knew Alex would be all right. I spent the next several minutes walking through the infirmary to check on my other patients and returned to find Alex wide-awake.

Best of all, he greeted me with his customary, "Hello, beautiful."

I replied, "Hello, Casanova" and checked his forehead. I found it cool.

He tried to sit up to drink, but fell back. "Damn," he said, "I'm as weak as a kitten."

I told him to go back to sleep so that I could get some work done.

He looked at me and said, "Lisette, I'm glad you are here."

I stayed on night duty for the next several nights and found myself enjoying it. The work was easier and I had time to sit and visit with the young wounded *Maquisards* and soldiers.

But as the September days shortened, I grew sad and restless. *Too many ghosts in my past*, I thought. The faces of my dead family and friends kept appearing in my dreams and I had nightmares about being tortured. Also, I missed Michelle, who still had not returned to duty. Depression was somewhat new to me, and I soon grew impatient with these feelings of despair. *The war is almost over*, I told myself; *I am strong and healthy. I should count myself fortunate to have survived.*

Because my workload was much lighter at night, I decided to find Marie and ask her to give me some extra assignments. The wounded had been unusually quiet and everyone seemed to be doing well. Marie said I could inventory our supplies.

The cool September air acted as a sleeping potion and I found it difficult to stay awake. I went outside for a few minutes hoping the evening air would make me more alert. It was peaceful outside and I thought: *How great to be alive!* My thoughts were of home and family and an early end to the war so that everyone could resume normal lives. *Would Maman forgive me for joining the Resistance or just think of me as the black sheep of the family? Why had I spend so much time in boarding schools, away from home and family? Why had Maman chosen to send me away while letting my brother and sisters remain at home?*

Yet, Maman could be very loving. I remembered my last holiday at home when Maman came into my room one evening, hugged me, and told me how much she loved me. *How good she had made me feel!* She talked about how she had sacrificed for me, and how sometimes she had made hard decisions but always in my best interests. "Sometimes," she said, "it is necessary to follow one's conscience and just do the right thing.

Courage — one must always have the courage to face the problems of life. Someday, when you are older, you will understand," she had concluded.

Only much later, after the war, did I finally discover what Maman had been trying to tell me. Only then did I learn that Maman and Papa had sent me away to boarding school to prevent me from acquiring tuberculosis, the disease that made Suzanne ill and claimed the life of my older sister, Annick.

My thoughts returned to the present and I went inside to begin the inventory. It was midnight and the patients would not need anything until about 3 o'clock. I listed everything we had on hand and straightened out the supply closet. The clock read 3:30 a.m. when I headed back upstairs to check on my patients. I heard scuffling noises and someone yelling as I entered the stairwell. I bounded upstairs, smelling smoke before I reached the top of the stairs.

"Mon Dieu, la maison est en feu!" — *Oh, my God, the house is on fire* — I yelled loudly.

Heavy smoke billowed from the alcove just right of the stairs, and I could already see tongues of fire eagerly lapping at the doorway to the big hall where the patients were housed. The fire threatened to block their escape. Some of the patients were already beating at the fire with their bedding. Andre, a young man who had lost his hand and shattered his arm when he had reached for an explosive, struggled to put the fire out. His legs and lungs were in good shape so I told him to go and get help.

Very quickly I realized that everyone must be evacuated as soon as possible because the fire was out of control. I directed those patients who could walk to help those who needed assistance. The smoke became almost suffocating. Yelling loudly, I told everyone to put wet towels to their faces to filter out the smoke.

The patients were amazingly calm. Those who were able supported those who needed help getting down the stairs. Alex appeared and together we helped an amputee make his way down the stairs on crutches. Dr. Soutille, Marie, and the medics arrived to help, but found the fire blazing out of control. Worse, the fire had blocked the escape of a number of patients. Annette, one of the nurses, led them to an alternate stairway but found it blocked by a collapsed wall.

I found a blanket and wet it down in the snow outside. Then I threw it over my head for one last attempt to reach some men in the back of the great hall. Some were ambulatory; others would require help to get out. I told those who could walk to join hands and follow me out, which they did without hesitation. As we worked our way through the curtain of fire, a large wooden beam supporting an inner wall collapsed. The beam brushed my shoulder just enough to knock me down the stairs. I had my breath knocked out and a slight burn on my arm, but I was not seriously injured. After the patients following me stopped to check on my condition, we all made our way out of the burning house without further incident.

The wind had switched and was blowing hard from the north, feeding the flames. The entire house was soon engulfed. I retreated to the courtyard where the patients had assembled and watched as the inferno raged, knowing not everyone could get out. I counted the patients, but could find only 37. On second count I still found only 37. Five were missing. I was devastated. *Who were they?*

I walked through the rows of patients trying to determine who remained inside. I missed Alex and nearly panicked. I knew he had gone outside, *but had he returned to help others?* I ran through the patients screaming, "Alex!" Then I saw Marie, who said he had been helping her just a few minutes earlier.

At that moment, I spotted him, walking unsteadily towards me. His face was scorched and he had a bandage around his head, but he was alive and smiling. He gathered me in his arms as I collapsed, crying uncontrollably. He kissed me on the forehead and looked into my face. "You've been so brave. No one could have done more. You can be proud of yourself," he told me quietly.

"Oh, Alex," I said, "I thought you were trapped inside."

He grinned and told me I looked kind of cute — *jolie* — with a black face. I laughed and remarked that he should see himself. "You have no eyebrows."

We silently clung to each other in the light of the burning building.

The house burned to the ground, and we never learned the source of the fire. We saved nothing except the clothes on our backs and the blankets patients had wrapped around themselves when they escaped the inferno. The infirmary moved into the forest and we camped out with only the shelter of the trees to protect us. We needed everything — food, medications, instruments, and other supplies. People from the surrounding countryside contributed what they could, but they had little to spare. It was late September and growing colder daily.

"What are we going to do?" I asked Dr. Soutille. "How can we care for patients without food or medication?"

Dr. Soutille assured me that the British were sending everything we needed. However, very soon, our Resistance unit would be disbanded and incorporated into the First French Army under General de Latter de Tassigny.

I asked Dr. Soutille when the supplies would be arriving, at the same time informing him that my patients were so hungry I could hardly look them in the face. When he replied the drop would take place very soon, I asked him to let me go along and help pick up the medical supplies. Dr. Soutille looked skeptical. "Please, I need to feel useful," I begged. He finally nodded in agreement.

Unfortunately, endless delays followed, and the drop did not take place until about a week after the fire. During the waiting period, we moved into an abandoned barn and used hay to provide some warmth for the patients, but they were all on starvation rations and our medications were almost exhausted. I began to feel guilty about eating anything at all. I tried not eating, but became so weak and tired I couldn't do my work. Finally, when arrangements for the drop were completed, Dr. Soutille whispered to me, "I'll come for you about 2 o'clock in the morning."

The contingent for picking up the airdropped supplies amounted to about a dozen trucks and more than 100 men. We drove in an ambulance for more than an hour before we came to a clearing in the forest and stopped. After assigning duties and making final preparations for the airdrop, we waited about ten minutes before we heard the sound of an airplane. That was our signal to light the torches, which we had placed in a circle about the size of a baseball field. Each of us hurried to light the torches in the area we had been assigned. The plane circled a time or two, then several parachutes with large bundles attached descended through the night sky.

Excitedly, we gathered up the packages like children at Christmas time. Blankets, medicine, guns, ammunition, and food of all kinds appeared, including apples, chocolate bars, and K-rations — the field rations originally designed by the U.S. Army for use by field troops. I wanted to both laugh and cry as I unwrapped the luxuries.

The next morning everyone in the camp awoke to the smell of freshly brewed coffee. We felt like celebrating as we watched the patients eat their first really nourishing meal in a long time.

By early October 1944, my life as a member of the Resistance was nearing an end. The French army was in the process of incorporating all *Maquis* units throughout France. Now, when I think back, the time I spent in the Resistance provided me with both very good and very bad memories. It was a difficult life, and there were certainly times when I wondered why I had chosen this primitive and dangerous existence over a relatively safe existence at home. Not only did I nearly lose my own life, but repeatedly I watched young boys and good men die, victims of the *Milice* or the Germans. On the other hand, I will never forget the close friends I made, such as Michelle and Alex. We developed a wonderful sense of camaraderie, strengthened by the hardships we shared, our conviction in the righteousness of our cause, and our hate for the Germans. And despite all the horror, my experiences in the Resistance has left me with some beautiful memories, some of which have been a source of comfort and strength throughout my life.

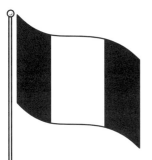

... My days at boot camp were probably the happiest of my young life, and I made up my mind to pursue a military career. ...

Chapter 10

ON OCTOBER 10, 1944, the *Maquis de l'Etang-Neuf (Yonne)* became the First Voluntary Regiment of Yonne. We were incorporated into the Second Moroccan Infantry Division, a part of the First French Army. Although our work continued as before, officially we were no longer in the Resistance. We were soldiers, and now received our pay through the French army rather than the Resistance. We were paid 20 French francs per month as members of the Resistance when funds were available from our leaders in England. Officially, I once again became Elisabeth Kapelian, but I continued to go by Lisette among my friends.

As soldiers, we were required to spend a few weeks at boot camp to undergo basic military training. Michelle and I were scheduled to attend the same camp together, then rejoin our unit in the Belfort area after we completed training.

The day before leaving for boot camp, I was winding up my duties

Iere Armée Française.
2eme DIVISION d'INFANTERIE MAROCAINE .
Ier Regiment de Volontaires de l' Yonne.
E.M./I.-773.

     Le Chef de bataillon ADAM, Commandant le Ier Reg. de Volontaires de l'Yonne, dans la Resistance chef adjoint au reseau "Jean-Marie", organisation de sabotages et de parachutages d'armes du circuit Buckmaster (war-Office) certifie que:
     KAPELIAN Elisabeth, née le 15.12.1924 à Larissa (grece)

a rejoint le reseau le I.6.1944 en qualité d'infirmiere attachée au maquis de l'Etang-neuf (Yonne), y restant jusqu'à la Liberation (28.8.1944) et s'engageant alors dans la IVeme I/2 Brigade de l' Yonne (devenue le IO.IO.1944 le Ier Regiment de Volontaires de l'Yonne).

    L'infirmiere Kapelian a toujours montré les plus belles qualités de courage et d'abnegation, donnant toujours, meme dans les circonstances les plus perilleuses, l'exemple de son sang-froid. Elle a rendu ainsi tant dans la Resistance qu'au regiment des services eminents.

    L'infirmiere Kapelian a été mutée au service de san. des A.F.A.T. de la Iere Armée le I5 Janvier 1945.

     à S.P. 50.054 le 3I Janvier 1945

    le Chef de Bataillon ADAM commandant le Ier R.V.Y

Above and opposite (translation): The year of Elisabeth Kapelian's birth is not correct on this citation from the First French Army, and was often misquoted in other military records. Her official birth certificate has been lost from the public record in Greece. To the best of her knowledge, she was born on December 15, 1927.

First French Army

The 2nd Moroccan Infantry Division

First Voluntary Regiment of Yonne

E.M./I.-773

    The Chief of the Battalion, Adam, Commander of the First Voluntary Regiment of Yonne in the Resistance, Joint Chief of the Reseau "Jean-Marie," organization of sabotage and parachuting of arms of the Buckmaster Network (War Office) certifies that Kapelian, Elisabeth born the 12/15/1924, Larissa. Greece/

    Joined the network 1/6/44 as a nurse and assigned to the maquis of Etang-Neuf (Yonne) and stayed until the liberation 8/28/1944. And then joined the Fourth 1/2 Brigade of Yonne which became the First Voluntary Regiment of Yonne 10/10/1944.

    Nurse Kapelian has always shown the most beautiful qualities of courage and sacrifice, giving always, even in the most perilous circumstance, without fear. <u>She distinguished herself as much in the Resistance as in the Regiment.</u>

    Nurse Kapelian was incorporated in the service of the A.F.A.T.(Women's Army Corps) of the First French Army on the 15th of January 1945.

                  To S.P. 50,054 31 January 1945

              The Chief of the Battalion Adam
              Commander of the First Voluntary Regiment of Yonne

                        Signature

                        Seal

Subscribed and sworn to before me this 18th *day of* Aug 1993
My commission expires Nov 1994

                     Notary Public

when I saw Alex watching me from the doorway to the infirmary. When I waved to him, he immediately came over and said he needed to talk to me. Naturally, I agreed.

We met at twilight under a chestnut tree right outside of camp. Alex had removed his black beret and was twisting it nervously when I arrived.

"What's so important?" I asked. "You seem so serious."

Alex replied that he just wanted to say good-bye since he had decided to go home instead of joining the army. "I left a girl at home," he said.

"Is her name Anna?"

He looked at me in amazement. "How could you know that? I haven't told anyone about Anna."

I joked by saying, "I'm a witch."

"I know," Alex smiled. "That is the reason I have to leave, you have bewitched me."

I looked at him, not really understanding what he was saying.

"I've grown to care for you too much over these past months," Alex continued. "I think I'm in love with you."

I looked at him for a moment as his words sank into my mind. Then I told him I also cared for him very much, but like a brother, not a lover.

"I understand, Lisette," he said. "I just wanted you to know I admire you and think you are brave and beautiful. I realize it can't go any further than this, but I hope you understand how I feel."

I stood on my tiptoes and we just held each other for awhile, knowing we might never see each other again. He told me he loved me and that part of him would always be with me.

"I love you too, Alex, you know that," I assured him. He walked me back to my quarters, kissed me on my cheek, and walked out of my life.

I would think of Alex frequently. Paradoxically, although we were very close, I really knew very little about him. I didn't even know where he lived. *What were his dreams? What would he do for a livelihood?* He richly deserved a happy life. I hoped and prayed that Alex and Anna would be happy the rest of their lives.

The next morning Michelle and I went by truck to an army camp for our training. The camp was located in eastern France, in the mountains between Dijon and Belfort. It was beautiful there, the air brisk and clean, and best of all, it seemed far away from the ugliness of the war.

A middle-aged woman greeted us and issued uniforms and equipment. We were shown to our dormitory, assigned bunks, and told to be in the

Elisabeth at boot camp, November 1944.

central barracks at 6 o'clock for dinner. The rest of the afternoon was ours to do whatever we pleased. Once we were alone, Michelle stretched out on the bunk and declared joyfully, "This is divine. Imagine, a whole bed, just for me." I suggested a nap, but Michelle was already asleep, snoring softly. She had not completely recovered from the pneumonia she had suffered in September.

I was glad to be alone. I needed time to think. I took my jacket and went for a walk on the mountain trails — beautiful with golden and amber trees. I loved walking on the crunchy fallen leaves. I wandered along the trail until just before dinner, when I returned to pick up Michelle. We went to dinner together where we had a rich country stew with chicken, vegetables, crusty French bread, and a smooth pudding for dessert.

"I feel like I've died and gone to heaven," Michelle remarked as we were walking back to our barracks.

"I know," I replied, "isn't it wonderful?" We arrived at our quarters and a young redhead was strumming the guitar and singing softly. We sat down beside her. I just enjoyed the music, but Michelle joined her in song. They harmonized beautifully. I was surprised by Michelle's lovely contralto voice.

The barracks was almost full of young women. Some had been members of the Resistance and some had not. Odette, the redhead, introduced us to her twin sister, Lucette. Although both were pretty, slightly plump, buxom, and almost identical in appearance, they were different in one important way. Odette's bust was decidedly larger than Lucette's, an obvious fact that became the subject of jokes at the camp. Also, their personalities were quite different. Lucette was introverted, and could be perfectly happy reading quietly by herself. However, the more gregarious Odette always enjoyed being the center of attention.

The days passed quickly and happily for us. Every morning except Sunday we were awakened by a bugle at 6 o'clock. We made our beds, then washed and dressed quickly for inspection. Breakfast consisted of coffee and a hard roll, after which we had calisthenics. Next, we usually went on a hike through the mountain trails with backpacks. We always sang as we hiked, usually a spirited marching song, but sometimes dirty songs about the Germans. After the hike, we had a simple nourishing lunch followed by afternoon classes. We learned how to discover mines, to read maps, and to understand some Morse code. We also received instruction on military regulations and emergency medical care.

Our lives were very structured, and we learned quickly there was trouble if orders were not followed correctly and promptly. Michelle and I both grew stronger and healthier with regular exercise and an adequate diet. Best of all, we had time for lots of girl talk, games, and indulging in luxuries, which had existed only in our dreams as members of the Resistance.

My days at boot camp were probably the happiest of my young life, and I made up my mind to pursue a military career. I would go to nurses' training after the war and then re-enter the French army as an *infirmiere*. For the first time in memory, I felt needed and rejoiced in the close relationships established at boot camp.

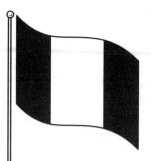

... By January 1945, ... war continued as usual. Many casualties, if not picked up and taken to a shelter very quickly after being wounded, froze to death where they had fallen.

Chapter 11

IN KEEPING WITH General Dwight D. Eisenhower's "broad-front" strategy, in November 1944 the Allies launched a general offensive all the way from the North Sea to Switzerland. In the Alsace-Lorraine sector, the burden of the attack, which began on November 14th, fell on the First French Army and the American Seventh Army.

On November 14th the First French Army under General de Lattre de Tassigny launched a major campaign in the southern part of Alsace, in the Belfort area. De Tassigny's mission was to drive through Alsace and push the Germans back to the Rhine River, which he did, but only after encountering strong German resistance. The progress of the French army was also hampered by numerous minefields, extreme cold, and heavy snow — up to four feet deep in some places. Nevertheless, after much bitter fighting, the First French Army breached the "Belfort Gap" and by November 19th had

Graduation from boot camp, November 1944.

pushed the Germans back to the Rhine. The French liberated Mulhouse on November 20th.

To the north, General LeClerc's Second Armored Division and the Seventh Army liberated Strasbourg on November 23rd. Afterward, Allied forces controlled the entire west bank of the Rhine from Strasbourg to the Swiss border except for the area around Colmar, known as the "Colmar Pocket," the only part of France still held by the Germans.[20]

By late November, with our boot camp training completed, Michelle and I reported to our duties near Belfort as scheduled, and were assigned to Hospital #42, of the First French Army, as nurses and ambulance drivers. We were serving front-line troops now, so our casualties were double that of the worst times in the *Maquis*.

Our hospital unit moved as the French army moved, north and east toward Mulhouse and eventually toward the frozen hell of Colmar. Casualties poured into the hospital by the hundreds daily. While many suffered wounds fighting against the Germans, we also treated many casualties caused by the cruel winter weather. The lack of adequate winter clothing made the situation even worse. Some of our soldiers had neither socks nor boots, and many lacked gloves. As a result, we treated many soldiers for frostbite, a condition which frequently required amputation of their hands or feet.

During the Christmas season, our hospital was in an old church. A stove, fueled by scraps of wood and small trees the orderlies had scrounged from the nearby woods, stood in the middle of the church. The Germans had long since stripped the area of the most readily accessible wood for their own needs. We placed the wounded as close as possible to the stove to keep them warm.

Most of our food was supplied by the Americans. Everything came in cans, but it was nourishing, filling, and for the most part satisfying. Whatever it was, we were always delighted to get it, even in cans.

Christmas 1944 was a lonely and sad time for all of us. I found myself crying for no reason and praying that the suffering and destruction of lives would end quickly. I kept thinking of home, especially the Christmases of my youth.

One Christmas, when I was eight years old, was particularly memorable. At that time, Suzanne was only five years old. Annick had been diagnosed with tuberculosis and spent the holidays in the sanitarium. Suzanne and I were playing in my room when Maman came in, her eyes gleaming with excitement. She exclaimed that she had just received a call from her sister who lived in New York City. "She is coming for Christmas, isn't it wonderful?"

Anything that could put Maman in such a good mood had to be wonderful. Everyone bustled around preparing for *Tata Marthe* — Aunt Marthe, whom Maman had not seen for more than ten years. Maman hummed while she worked in the kitchen, making her wonderful pastries for the joyous occasion. Papa stayed busy treating his patients with all the usual winter diseases, but he also seemed pleased about the coming visit.

I remembered how he would walk into the house carrying his big black doctor's bag and go straight to the kitchen, where Maman seemed to spend all her time. He blew warm air on his cold fingers first, then brushed the tendrils that escaped from Maman's chignon and kissed her on the back of the neck. He lifted the lid of whatever was cooking on the stove and remarked about how good it smelled.

Maman's reply never varied. "Go see about the children and make sure that everyone is washed up; then we will have dinner."

I remembered how anxious Maman had been to have everything perfect for Tata Marthe. Papa brought flowers, which Suzanne and I were to present to her when we were introduced for the first time.

The train pulled into the station and I watched as all the passengers stepped off. Then Maman screamed and ran over to a very large woman who was scanning the crowd with a distasteful look on her face, as though she had just gotten a whiff of something that smelled bad. I disliked her on sight.

When I was introduced, Tata Marthe pinched me on the cheek instead of kissing me. I hated the greeting, but I smiled, curtsied, and handed her the flowers anyway. We gathered Tata's luggage and headed for home. We sat down to the dinner that Maman had been preparing for days. Tata Marthe looked at it, sniffed, and said she could not eat rich food anymore; it gave her indigestion. But I noticed she filled her plate twice and ate two servings of dessert.

After dinner, Tata went to her room and we didn't see her for two days. Everyone had to be very quiet because she was very tired. I read the book that Tata had brought from America, *La Case de l'Oncle Tom — Uncle Tom's Cabin*, by Harriet Beecher Stowe. I was fascinated by the poor black slaves and cried and cried about poor little Eva and Topsy. At least Tata had brought me an excellent book.

I grew restless and asked Maman if I could listen to the radio. While I was listening Maman scolded me for having the volume too high. She bribed me to be quiet by promising me I could attend Midnight Mass at Notre Dame. The adults in my family had always attended Midnight Mass on Christmas at Notre Dame. Although I didn't know the details, I suspect that our seats were acquired by Grandpere who was a well-known contractor in Villeneuve St. Georges and contributed generously to the Catholic Church.

Christmas Eve arrived and I was on my best behavior all day. I felt excited about going to Midnight Mass and did not want to jeopardize my opportunity in any way. We left for the cathedral early. Grandmere and Grandpere went with us, as did Aunt Celine and Uncle Armand. The other children had been left at home, which made me feel very grown-up.

Notre Dame was absolutely beautiful. The Christmas tree was decorated with fruit and ribbons, and a manger had been set up near the altar with real people portraying Mary, Joseph, and little baby Jesus. There were animals nearby: a cow, two sheep, a dog, and a cat. But baby Jesus cried and cried. I asked Maman why baby Jesus cried so much.

She answered, "Because he is cold and very poor."
"Can I give baby Jesus my bonbons?"
"No! Be quiet."

I tried to take my hat off; it was new and caused my head to itch. Maman became cross with me so Grandmere let me sit next to her and Grandpere. Grandmere held my hand as we sat together. I still remembered the warm feeling we shared that night. I knew I was Grandmere's favorite and I loved her unconditionally.

I grew bored listening to all the singing, which I did not understand. Baby Jesus kept crying and crying. Maman went up front for communion and the service eventually came to an end, but we still stood in line a long time to kiss the hand of the priest. When it was my turn, the priest smiled and said, "You are a mature young lady." Then he handed me some candy and oranges.

When we arrived home, Papa and Maman disappeared into the parlor to see if Papa Noel had arrived while we were at church. Of course, I was too old to believe that Papa Noel actually went all over the world on his donkey, delivering presents to good little children. But Suzanne believed, so I kept the secret.

I woke Suzanne and we all went into the parlor. The Christmas tree was beautiful, all aglow with candles and decorated with apples, oranges, and tinsel. Tata Marthe had given me a pencil and some American chocolate, which I disliked. Papa gave me a gold coin and a book, *Le dernier des Mohicans — The Last of the Mohicans*. I received a pretty silver comb from Maman.

We gathered in the dining room for our Christmas supper called the *reveillon*. Maman had prepared fish and turkey stuffed with chestnuts. Everyone had champagne, even Suzanne and I, although ours was heavily diluted with water. The next morning, we slept late, and around noon relatives began arriving. Grandmere and Grandpere brought Annick home from the sanitarium to spend the day. She looked very pale, but her cough was better and she seemed happy to be home.

Aunts, uncles, and lots of cousins came to see Tata Marthe. Everyone brought food and we had a bountiful dinner; then the adults went to the parlor to talk and the children played. We were having a wonderful time playing hide-and-seek when Tata Marthe stuck her head in the door and said sternly, "Please be quiet, you've given me a splitting headache."

Papa was just behind her and politely asked her to leave us alone. We were only having fun and it was Christmas. I remember how proud I was of Papa at that moment. He winked at me as Tata stormed off to her room and slammed the door. Charles, my 11-year-old cousin, was very mature but easily intimidated. He whispered that we had better be quiet or she would get us into trouble. But only a few minutes later, I saw Tata Marthe heading for the dining room where she had more dessert, so I figured she couldn't feel too bad.

Tata Marthe left to go back to America the next Sunday. As she was leaving, she pinched my cheek again and said, "When you are a little bigger you must visit me in America."

I stood up to my full height and replied, "I will never visit you in America because I don't like to be pinched."

I smiled at the memories as I became fully awake and looked around at reality. I was seated on the cold church floor with wounded men all around me. They didn't complain about the cold because they knew we were doing all we could. It was Christmas and I wanted so much to make their pain go away, so I suggested to Michelle we all sing carols. Michelle smiled and began singing "Silent Night" in her lovely, rich, contralto voice. The soldiers joined in, then the orderlies, and the doctors. There were tears in everyone's eyes as we sang our favorite Christmas songs, celebrating the birth of Christ.

By January 1945, the weather had improved, but it was still bitterly cold. The snow stopped for awhile but a dense fog and heavy mist hung over the landscape, giving the appearance of a dream — or a nightmare. The war continued as usual. Many casualties, if not picked up and taken to a shelter very quickly after being wounded, froze to death where they had fallen.

Although slowly being driven out of France, the German army still had enough strength to mount one last major attack. On December 31, 1944, the Germans hurled eight divisions against the unsuspecting American Seventh Army and the First French Army in the Alsace-Lorraine sector. Known as *Operation Northwind* and planned in part by Hitler personally, the attack aimed primarily at the retaking of Strasbourg. After hard fighting, however, the Allies successfully defended the city and then gradually resumed offensive operations. They liberated Colmar on February 2nd, eliminated the pocket by the 9th, and continued to advance until the Germans fell back to the east bank of the Rhine.[21]

Sometimes I thought the primary enemy during this bitter winter was not the Germans, but the cold, the snow, and the fog. At our hospital, soldiers with frozen limbs outnumbered the wounded-in-action by two to one. We became masters at improvising to keep the cold from claiming even more victims. The nurses put frozen morphine ampules under their armpits to thaw and warmed plasma by placing it on a stove in a can or under the hoods of ambulances. Because we had few blankets, the nurses and orderlies heated bricks in the stove and wrapped them in towels so that the wounded could use them as a heat source. We dried wet socks and gloves by placing them in cans of heated pebbles. We also inserted the pebbles into wet shoes and boots.

Odette and Lucette, the pretty red-haired twins I had met in boot camp, joined us at the hospital. They were several years older than me and had been nurses before the war. They worked as a team, like Michelle and I. Odette worked as a nurse while Lucette drove the ambulance. Odette became very popular with the soldiers because of her sweet, outgoing personality. She began massaging the feet of the patients at night to prepare them for sleep. I took up the habit and found the massage warmed my hands as much as the patients' feet.

I liked having Odette and Lucette around. Odette was lively and fun. Lucette was quieter and more thoughtful, but possessed a dry wit which she revealed at unexpected and stressful times. They were like peas in a pod with their beautiful green eyes and flaming red hair. The soldiers liked them and never tired of guessing which pretty twin they were talking to.

Michelle and I went out in the ambulance every day to pick up the wounded and transport them back to the hospital. On one particularly cold morning, as we loaded up to return to camp, I heard someone calling for help. Michelle almost convinced me it was only the wind whipping through the trees. The dense fog restricted visibility to, at most, only a few feet. As we prepared to leave, I heard it again: an eerie voice calling in French for help. It sounded like a woman or child and I wouldn't leave until I checked it out. I trudged through the snow to a small thicket of trees and found a young German soldier, out of his mind with pain. His right leg had been blown off at the knee, probably by a mine. He would have bled to death if the severe cold had not stopped the flow of blood. When I bent

Elisabeth Kapelian, *circa* 1945.

down to check him over, he grabbed my hand and started crying and babbling in French. I could not understand what he was saying but I responded in French, *"Tout Va . . . bien. Je vais vous aider"* — everything is alright . . . I am going to help you.

"*Merci, merci beaucoup*," he sobbed.

We loaded him into the ambulance and I gave him a shot of morphine to dull his pain. When we arrived back at the hospital and I took my first real look at him, my heart almost stopped. He looked a lot like Norbert, the handsome altar boy at the boarding school. He had clear blue eyes, blond hair, and a young face as smooth as that of a baby, without even a hint of a beard. He slept continuously, but always awoke in a good mood and a smile.

Like so many in the German army late in the war, he was young, only 15 years old, and had been in the military only a few weeks. I remember his name was Wolfgang, and I couldn't resist the trust he placed in me. He seemed to be frightened by thoughts of how his captors might treat him simply because he was German.

Wolfgang seemed happy to be safe and sheltered and always appreciated our care. He had an enormous appetite and ate every morsel of food on his plate. I had seen German prisoners before but they had been surly and defiant. Wolfgang had a gentle nature, and even the amputation of his right leg above the knee and part of his left foot did not make him bitter. French, I learned, was his first language; his French mother had taught it to him when he was a baby.

Michelle and Odette felt very hostile towards Wolfgang, so as compensation for their attitudes, I tried to be extra nice to him. When he was out of danger, he was transferred to a prison camp nearby. I hope he was treated with kindness.

After meeting Wolfgang, I looked at the war from a different viewpoint. This young German boy was a war victim also. He should have been home, attending school and flirting with girls of his own age, but instead he was maimed for life.

We soon moved to another location. Because we traveled so slowly, the ambulances and hospital crews always brought up the rear. We established our new hospital in an old run-down house just outside a small village. There was no stove, so we made our own. The orderlies gathered stones and whatever wood they could find, then placed the stones, with the wood on top, in the middle of the largest and most protected room. The burning wood heated the stones, which became very hot and warmed the room for hours.

The fighting intensified. The Germans apparently had brought up reinforcements and were determined to stop the Allied advance. And to make matters worse, the snow started again.

One day Michelle and I, plus a paramedic whose name I cannot remember, were sent to pick up some wounded near the front. We experienced some difficulty reaching our destination, but the snow seemed to be letting up as twilight fell. We loaded our patients, three Frenchmen and one German officer, and started back to camp. One of the French soldiers had a bullet in his chest and was bleeding profusely. I gave him morphine to ease his pain, then went to work to stop the flow of blood. He was in real danger of bleeding to death before we reached the hospital, and I told Michelle she needed to drive as fast as possible. The paramedic took care of the other patients.

Soon, I became aware that we were barely moving. Michelle, I discovered, was frantically wiping the windshield with her gloved hand. It was pitch dark and snowing heavily again and Michelle could not see the road. I climbed into the front seat and saw that visibility was zero; we were traveling blindly. I cautioned Michelle to keep moving so we didn't freeze. Michelle agreed, but added that she had no idea which direction we were going.

Because the windshield wipers did not work, Michelle tried clearing the window by reaching outside and wiping away the layer of ice with her hand as she drove. When this didn't work, we stopped the ambulance, and the paramedic got out and attempted to scrape away the ice, but with little success. He did clear away some ice from the headlights, so at least we had a dim light ahead of us. Shivering, the paramedic jumped back into the ambulance and reported that Michelle would have to drive with the window open in order to see anything at all. "Furthermore," he added, "we are off the road"; there were tire tracks several feet to our right.

Michelle turned the ambulance in the direction he pointed and we were soon on the road again, but we didn't know which direction we were going. The French soldier with the chest wound began convulsing and stopped breathing as I worked desperately to resuscitate him. The paramedic joined Michelle in the front seat as we inched our way through the blinding snowstorm. None of us were aware that the sound of artillery was growing louder until a shell exploded nearby. Michelle stopped and began turning the ambulance around. "We are getting too close to the combat zone!" the paramedic shouted. Another shell hit just yards away, lighting up the austere landscape. *At least*, I thought, *we could see the road clearly for a few seconds.*

Michelle turned the ambulance around and we headed in the opposite direction. She drove almost blind as the snow and sleet tapped at the windshield, stinging our faces as we struggled to see out of the open windows. The windshield had a thick layer of ice that nothing could penetrate. The paramedic tried to direct her by shining the flashlight on the landscape as he rode with his head out the window.

Suddenly, a blinding light illuminated everything. I heard nothing, but I felt myself being lifted into the air and slammed against something hard. And then I felt nothing. When I opened my eyes again, it was dark. I knew from the familiar sounds around me I was in a hospital. I could remember being in the ambulance in the driving snow, but nothing else. I wanted Michelle.

Odette was sitting by my cot when I awoke. It was early in the morning and still dark and cold. I asked, "Where am I?"

Odette replied that I was back in the hospital. "You have a concussion and shrapnel over your head and body, but you are going to be fine," she told me.

"But what happened?" I queried. I tried to sit up but excruciating pain shot through my head and into my back.

Odette explained that our ambulance had been hit by mortar fire. We had wandered into the combat zone and got caught in the crossfire.

"Oh, yes," I remembered, "Michelle was trying to turn the ambulance around. Michelle? Where is she?"

"She died instantly," Odette replied. "She couldn't have known what hit her."

When I realized what had happened, I cried, long and hard. My head hurt badly, but the emptiness I felt inside hurt worst. Odette gave me a shot of morphine and I drifted back to sleep. The next few days were a nightmare for me. I felt fine as long as I lay still, but moving my head caused terrible headaches.

All I could do was to lay there and think. And the more I thought, the more depressed I became. *Why Michelle?* I thought of the first time we had met. We were on the truck escaping the Paris Gestapo. *How shy and intense she had seemed!* Poor Michelle had always thought she would never survive the war. But since boot camp she had seemed more optimistic, more self-assured. More tears came to my eyes as I thought of the happy times we had shared. I would always remember the pleasant surprise of hearing her beautiful singing voice. We had shared so much. *And now she is gone.*

I learned that all the French soldiers in the ambulance were killed by the mortar shell; the German officer had survived, but the paramedic was in a critical condition. Over and over, I thought about all the family and friends I had lost. *Why had I been spared?* After several days in bed, my headaches improved and I was allowed to get up for a few hours at a time, but I was so dizzy I was useless in the hospital. My wounds were healing and I wanted more than anything else to go back to work.

Dr. Soutille stopped by to see how I was doing. He told me he wanted me to take some time off. "You need time to recuperate — get your strength back," he advised.

I protested: " I will be better soon and would rather go directly back to work."

Dr. Soutille, however, remained firm, "Lisette," he said, "you need to get away. You are not well yet. A week of sleep and good food and maybe a little fun will make you a better nurse. That's an order."

Toward the end of January 1945, I reluctantly boarded a train to Paris. I was so tired I could hardly keep my eyes open. *At least*, I thought, *Paris would have plenty of comfortable beds,* and I fully intended to find one and sleep for a week. I felt guilty, knowing I was going to Paris with no plans to visit Maman. However, going home would mean answering endless questions, which I was in no mood to do. I was just not yet ready to listen to Maman's certain reproof of my Resistance activities. What my mind and body needed was to forget about things for awhile and just relax.

Dr. Soutille had suggested that I spend my time at the Scribe Hotel, which was open to all Allied forces. No matter where I was, I could not stop thinking about Michelle — beautiful Michelle, who had shared all her dreams and hopes with me since we first met as members of the *Maquis.* Somehow, with Michelle around, all the horrors of the war seemed tolerable. We could always find something to laugh about even under the most dismal conditions. I wept silently as I recalled our days together, while the train rolled on toward Paris.

The train arrived at the Gare de l'Est and I took a taxi to the Scribe Hotel located on Rue Scribe near the Opera and La Madeleine. The hotel lobby was beautiful, with dark wood paneling and marble floors covered with fine oriental carpets. I checked into my room and went straight to the dining room for a light supper of a delicious, rich soup with crusty French bread and real butter.

Then I went back to my room for a long sleep. My room was lovely in shades of blue with touches of white. It contained a large four-poster bed, a bureau, and dresser with a mirror. In a little alcove was a pretty little settee and two dainty chairs around a table in front of a large window. I hung my spare blouse in the armoire and put my few belongings in the drawers. The other door in the room revealed a private bath with a huge footed tub. How wonderful it looked as I disrobed and stepped into a steaming hot bath. *How long had it been since I had relaxed in a real bathtub of hot water?* It seemed like I had walked into another life.

I washed my hair, scrubbed my tired body, and just relaxed in the tub until the water cooled. I was pulling my nightshirt over my head when someone knocked on the door. A smiling, older woman stood at my door with a bottle of champagne in one hand and a bouquet of red roses in the other. "Mademoiselle Kapelian?" she inquired.

I nodded yes, thanked her, and accepted the champagne and roses. I quickly discovered a note in the flowers from my friends at the hospital telling me to have a wonderful time. *How kind they are*, I thought, as I wiped tears from my eyes.

There was something about war, perhaps the fragility of life, that made one feel close to friends. So many of my good friends had died in the past months. I had become wary of making more close relationships. Still, it kept happening over and over. Just barely 18, I already felt old and tired.

What more could one ask than to be warm and dry? I watched the wind bend the trees outside and icy rain pelt my window. My first sip of champagne tasted delightful — cold, slightly sweet, and bubbly. The bubbles tickled my nose as I drank. I finished my first glass and poured another. The champagne made me dizzy but delightfully warm inside. I felt sophisticated as I sipped my champagne in my beautiful hotel room. It even occurred to me that I might enjoy my time on leave.

When sunlight woke me the next morning, the light hurt my eyes and I felt slightly nauseated. However, after showering and dressing, I felt much better. I was very hungry by the time I reached the dining room. I had breakfast and was drinking coffee when I noticed that only one other person was eating, a young woman. Our eyes met and she got up and came over to my table. She introduced herself as Charlotte and asked if she could join me. I was happy to have a companion so I invited her to sit down.

Charlotte was pretty, with brown hair and beautiful, large, hazel eyes. She was petite, like myself, just an inch or two above five feet. She told me that she was a French army nurse and was on leave for a few days. I told her about myself and she laughed saying, "Wouldn't you know the only people in this place would be two hungry nurses?"

We both laughed. I found myself really enjoying her company. Charlotte was older and had been a *Sage-femme* (nurse-midwife) before the war. She was from Verdun and had never been to Paris.

We liked each other immediately despite the difference in our ages. I really admired her sense of humor. Charlotte found something funny in every situation. She told me I looked like her baby sister who was eight years younger. "My sister is the biggest nuisance in the world," she said. "Even worse, she's getting so beautiful she is taking all my boyfriends away, so watch yourself." Then Charlotte laughed that wonderful infectious laugh and I couldn't help from doing the same.

On the first day together, we shopped and went sightseeing. We spent a pleasant afternoon trying on ridiculous hats and giggling like small school girls. Though we were required to wear our uniforms at all times during our leave, we tried on the small selection of pretty dresses available in our sizes. Then we made up stories about what we would do in such dresses after the war. We both purchased new underwear and perfume.

When we arrived back at the hotel, we went to my room and trimmed each other's hair. Charlotte swept my long black hair up and trimmed my bangs. I liked the effect. At last, it was time for dinner and both of us were starving since we had missed lunch. We had a wonderful dinner at the hotel and enjoyed a second dessert with *café au lait* — coffee with hot milk. I looked up and happily told Charlotte that I had long dreamed of food like that.

Charlotte suggested that we go to the USO at the Ritz Hotel to meet some new people and have some fun. We decided to go to our rooms, get ready, and meet in the lobby at 10 o'clock We walked to the Ritz and found a large room filled with young men and women in uniform, laughing and dancing. Charlotte ordered a glass of champagne and I ordered a lemonade. I was not in the mood for liquor after consuming the whole bottle of champagne the previous night.

After watching the dancers for awhile, I touched Charlotte's hand and sheepishly told her, "I have a problem." I did not know how to dance. I had never learned.

Charlotte laughed and said, "You really are a baby, aren't you? It's simple, just watch for a moment." Then she explained how a man walks to the music and the woman just follows. As the man moves forward, the woman moves backwards.

I told Charlotte it looked complicated, and she patted my hand to reassure me. "You are young, fresh, and pretty," she said, "and any one of these men would love holding you in his arms and moving to the music. And you had better get ready, because your first partner is headed your way."

I looked up and a young American lieutenant stood at my elbow. He smiled at me and held out his arm. Charlotte said he wanted to dance with me. I stood up; he was a head taller than I and had blue-green eyes. I felt self-conscious, but I followed him to the dance floor. He had short, straight blond hair and a small mustache, which was a shade lighter than his hair. He was very handsome.

We seemed to move well together. Dancing seemed very natural to me and I followed his lead effortlessly. The music stopped and I turned and headed back to my table, but he grabbed my hand and stopped me. He said something that I did not understand, but his meaning was clear. He wanted me to stay and dance with him again. Soon we were dancing to the strains of "*Besame Mucho,*" a popular Wold War II song. The steps were a little more complicated to this music, but I caught the rhythm quickly. The slight pressure on my back and the way he held me signaled in advance where he would move next.

He kept looking at me, always grinning a cute lopsided grin, like he couldn't believe I was there. He smelled wonderful, musky with fresh lemony undertones. I found it delightful to be in his arms. I tried to speak to him, but it was obvious that he didn't understand French and I knew very little English.

Suddenly, in the middle of our dance, another soldier tapped him on his shoulder and I found myself in someone else's arms. I danced several dances with other partners, but I did not feel as comfortable with them as with my first partner. Finally I held up my hands to signal I was tired and went back to my table where Charlotte sat talking to an American captain. When I sat down, she told me, "You sure caught on to that little game quickly." I was tired but happy. I had never had so much fun.

Just then, the American lieutenant touched my arm, and in terrible French, asked me to dance again. I answered "*Oui,*" without hesitation.

I felt tingly and happy to see him again. The band began playing "*Besame Mucho*" again and I looked at him in surprise.

"They're playing our song again," he told me, in bad French, while grinning and looking at his English-French phrase book.

I smiled, trying to express with my eyes how flattered he made me feel. He tightened his hold on me and kissed me lightly on the cheek.

We finished the dance and went back to the table. Charlotte was still there, talking to the captain. She introduced us to Captain Samuel Morse, a pilot from Houston, Texas. Fortunately, Sam spoke a little French and Charlotte spoke some English, so we were able to converse a little, and had a marvelous time. The two soldiers shook hands and introduced themselves. I heard the lieutenant's name for the first time, James Hubert Randall from St. Paul, Minnesota. I introduced myself and for the next few minutes we experimented with each other's names. We had a wonderful time trying to figure out what the others were saying.

Before I knew it, the lights were blinking and the band was playing "Goodnight Sweetheart." We could not believe it was already 2 o'clock. After making plans with James and Sam for the next day, Charlotte and I walked back to our hotel and to our rooms. My head was swimming with thoughts of James and the strange and wonderful evening I had just experienced. *James has everything*, I thought. *He is handsome, intelligent, funny, and very sweet.* I could hardly wait for the morning to come.

It was a warm, beautiful day for our tour of Paris, with a bright, shining sun. Since I was familiar with the city, I served as the tour guide. Although ordered by Hitler, Paris was not destroyed during the occupation and I could show my new friends all the wonderful sites of the City of Light. I chose a peaceful garden area, the Place des Voges as our first stop. I explained to them, "Victor Hugo, the famous 19th-century author, often came here for inspiration."

I could see that James and Sam did not understand what I was talking about, but they listened politely. Suddenly, James leaned over and kissed me full on the lips. I felt overwhelmed by the sweetness and tenderness of his kiss, but also a little frightened.

As we wandered through the beautiful small park, we forgot about the war. Nothing existed for us except each other. We laughed and teased each other and developed a common language filled with expressions, hand signals, and a few common words.

Next, we decided to go back to the hotel for lunch. Charlotte laughed at me because I seemed to have lost my appetite. "Ma Petite, are you in love?" she teased.

I blushed, but did not deny it.

After lunch, we went to a French movie where James picked up some useful phrases. He had a quick, intelligent mind and a talent for language.

That night, we went dancing again. This time, I danced only with James. We moved as though in a dream that only had room for the two of us.

The next day, I arranged for the hotel to pack a picnic lunch for four and we all went to Montmartre where we could enjoy a marvelous view of Paris. It was cold when we arrived so I took them into the Basilica du Sacre Coeur. After touring the beautiful church, it was warmer outside, and we walked around the artists' colony to work up an appetite. We found a patch of sunshine and spread our blanket on La Place du Tertre.

We had great fun unloading the basket to see what delicacies the hotel had prepared for us. There were four baguettes with ham, cheese, vegetables, mustard, and pickles. James chose the largest. He started eating at one end and encouraged me to begin on the other end. After much laughter, we met in the middle and had a very tasty kiss.

It grew colder after lunch and all four of us played word games. Sam and James wrote sentences in English and Charlotte and I wrote sentences in French. James was the most inventive. It seemed that he had developed quite a vocabulary from the French movie we had seen the day before. We all rolled with laughter at his fake French accent and absurd expressions. He mimicked some phrases that held no meaning to him. This made them twice as funny when Charlotte and I translated.

The cold weather finally prompted us to return to the hotel. James and I sat in the lobby where he began showing me pictures of his parents and sister. The next few days went by far too quickly. The four of us spent almost every waking hour together. We walked down the Champs Elysées and paused and reflected at the Tomb of the Unknown Soldier under the

Arc de Triomphe. We went to the Comedie Francaise to see a play, Moliere's *Les Femmes Savantes*, and we danced every night. It was a beautiful, magic time for all of us.

With only two days of leave left, Charlotte came to my room and asked if I would mind if she and Sam spent the next day alone. Of course, I did not mind and I told her James and I could also use some time alone.

Charlotte then asked, "Do you know that James is seriously in love with you?"

I told her that I was aware of his feeling for me and that I thought I was also in love with him. I thought this was the way love was supposed to happen, but I really didn't know because I had never been in love before.

Charlotte reminded me that we were in wartime and feelings were often hurried and intensified during such times. It would make much more sense for us to take our time and get to know each other better, but she admitted this was not possible under the circumstances. "I really think you should enjoy each other while you can and let the future take care of itself," she counseled.

I thanked Charlotte for her advice. I was struck with how close we'd become in only a few days.

Charlotte started towards the door, looked back, and told me not to expect too much, "James is a young, healthy male very far from home and you are young, beautiful, and loving. But remember, you come from two different worlds."

I sat, staring at my reflection in the mirror for a long time after Charlotte left. *She was right, of course. James was much too appealing not to have been in love before. He probably had a girl at home and missed her very much.* But I decided I would love him now. I had to stop hoping for the future and live for the present.

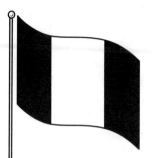

. . . How quickly and totally the war had passed from my mind during the past several days. I lived completely in the present with no thoughts of the past or immediate future.

Chapter 12

JAMES WAS SITTING at the breakfast table when I entered the hotel dining room. As soon as he saw me he smiled, stood up, and helped me into my seat. *"Bonjour cherie,"* he said cheerfully.

"Good morning, James," I replied. I noticed a thin, oblong package beautifully wrapped with silver paper and tied with a gold ribbon on the table beside his coffee. My eyes were drawn to it time and time again. *What did it contain? Was it for me?* Each time James saw me looking at it, he smiled and said nothing.

While we waited for breakfast, James pulled out a map of France and asked me where I would like to go for a day. He had borrowed a jeep which we could use until midnight. I was beginning to understand more and more English but it still took me a few minutes to figure out what he had said. James patiently explained to me in the most elementary sign language until I finally understood.

Without the slightest hesitation, I pointed to Fontainebleau, about 60 kilometers south of Paris. I wanted him to see the magnificent palace in the center of town so that he might enjoy the proud history of France. James smiled and nodded approvingly. I think I could have picked any place on the map and he would have reacted the same way. I left to ask the hotel manager to prepare a picnic basket for us to share while at Fontainebleau.

When I returned, James was sitting at a small table by the window, staring into space. He didn't see me approach, so I sneaked up and put my hands over his eyes. "Guess who." I said.

He chuckled and replied, "Solange? Charlotte? Colette?"

I laughed and pulled my hands away. James clasped my hand and kissed each finger, one by one, and then my palm. I sat down in the chair opposite him. He handed the package to me and watched my face as I opened it. Inside were the most beautiful leather gloves I had ever seen. I ran my fingers over their satiny texture. I told him how beautiful they were and thanked him. The glow in my eyes told him how much I liked them.

"Please try them on," he asked.

I picked the left one up first and slipped my hand into the glove. The lining was soft and warm. But something obstructed my progress; I couldn't get my fingers all the way into the glove. I struggled to free the small object which was stuck in one of the fingers. At last, when it came free, I saw what it was and gasped.

A lovely gold ring with a small solitary diamond sparkled as I held it carefully in the palm of my hand. My eyes filled with tears when I realized that it was an engagement ring. I looked at James whose own eyes were moist and shiny as he watched me.

"*Je t'aime, cherie*," he said as he slipped the ring on my finger. "I want you to marry me."

Then he faltered as he struggled to recall his memorized words, but they would not come. Finally, he reached into his pocket and handed me a note. I read the carefully constructed French phrases he had just tried to recite to me. I didn't need the note to understand what he had said, but I read it anyway to make sure I wasn't dreaming.

I thought my heart would burst with happiness and I threw my arms around his neck and shouted, *"Oui, Oui, mon cheri je serais heureuse d'etre ta femme pour toujours" — I would be happy to be your wife forever!* The ring fit and I couldn't stop looking at it, turning it to the light one way and then another to see how the lovely diamond captured the light and changed colors. So many thoughts, which I could not express in English, raced through my head. *What a wonderful feeling,* I thought, *to know we loved each other and were committed to a life together.* We smiled, laughed, and hugged each other until the manager appeared and informed us our lunch was ready.

"I must make a call first," I told James and I pointed to the telephone. James gestured to me that he would bring the jeep around front as he took the picnic basket and pointed to the front door.

I pulled on my new gloves as I crawled into the seat next to James. He asked me whom I had called and I told him it was to be a surprise. On our way to Fontainebleau I taught James some French songs. To my delight, he already knew parts of "Alouette" and "Frere Jacques." The February day was cold but sunny and bright, and we really didn't feel the cold. We just enjoyed being alone together.

We arrived at Fontainebleau and strolled through the beautiful palace. I found an English brochure that explained its history, and James eagerly devoured its contents. He seemed impressed to be strolling through the palace where Napoleon had abdicated and so many French kings had lived during the summers. I pronounced the names of the kings and queens who called it home and pointed to their pictures in the brochure. He tried to imitate my pronunciation, which usually prompted a good laugh from both of us.

James seemed proud that an American, John D. Rockefeller, had given France almost $3 million in the 1920s to restore Fontainebleau and other historical monuments. We had fun with our English-French brochures and made it a game to understand the other's language. And every few minutes I looked down admiringly at my sparkling diamond to make sure it was real and not just something I had dreamed.

Gray clouds obliterated the sun as we toured the grounds. It started getting even colder and a few flakes of snow fell from the darkening sky. James kissed me on the nose and whenever he felt me shiver, he hugged me tightly. By sign language, he indicated that he was hungry. He took me by the hand and we ran to the jeep where he retrieved the picnic basket from the back. First, we opened our thermos and drank steaming cups of hot coffee to warm us. Then he opened an excellent Bordeaux, poured the wine into the glasses, and we toasted our happiness.

After lunch, we went to a charming old church where we walked around and admired the workmanship of artists from centuries past. While we were in the church, I took a few minutes for prayer and gave thanks for my good fortune in meeting this wonderful man. When we came out, we found that a lovely soft snowfall had covered everything like a sifting of powdered sugar.

As we settled in the jeep, I directed James to our next destination. We traveled a few kilometers north until we entered the small, charming village of Villeneuve St. Georges. We drove to the Rue des Balkans where I told James to stop and park. We were at my grandparents' home. This was the surprise I had arranged for James.

A tiny woman, Grandmere stood dressed in black as usual, holding her large white handkerchief in her hand ready for the happy tears that were already forming in her eyes. Grandpere stood beside her, only slightly taller than Grandmere. I introduced James, who kissed Grandmere on the cheek and shook Grandpere's hand warmly. Grandmere put her arms around James and told him in English that they were happy to have him visit. However, for the time being she "would reserve judgment about our engagement because Elisabeth is so very young."

James had never heard me called Elisabeth before since I had always used Lisette. I explained about my work with the French Resistance and the necessity for using code names. Grandmere translated for us.

It was getting colder so we went directly into their house, laughing and happy as we entered. The wonderful smell of roast chicken and fresh bread wafted from the kitchen. Grandpere gave both of us a cup of hot spiced wine. I couldn't help but laugh when I heard Grandpere ask Grandmere if she was sure I was old enough to drink wine. Grandmere laughed and told Grandpere that if I were old enough to defend the country, then I was old enough to drink wine. Grandmere translated all this to James who stood and beamed at the obvious affection between the three of us.

We had a wonderful dinner and with Grandmere interpreting, I learned many things about James. He was 27 years old and had worked as a stockbroker in Minnesota before the war. A graduate of the University of Minnesota, he had one sister, Andrea. He loved to ride horses, sail, and to read anything he could find.

After dinner, James called his mother and father to inform them of our engagement. Grandmere spoke with James's parents and I briefly greeted them. They seemed pleased that James had found a girl he loved so much.

After we had completed the call, Grandmere and I sat down to talk while James and Grandpere sat in the living room smoking Turkish cigarettes and drinking wine. I explained to Grandmere the reasons why I had decided not to go home. I asked her not to mention my visit to Maman because it would only make her feel bad. Grandmere told me not to worry and assured me she would comply with my wishes.

The time flew by and we had to return the jeep by midnight. James and I bid our farewells to Grandmere and Grandpere and began our journey back to Paris. We arrived at the hotel about 11 o'clock and James left to return the jeep to his friend. I was very tired, but happy, and went directly to my room. I was surprised to find Charlotte waiting for me. She was smoking a cigarette and obviously had been crying.

"What's wrong?" I asked.

Charlotte looked up and stroked my cheek, remarking that I looked radiant.

I thrust out my left hand so Charlotte could see the engagement ring. "We are engaged. Isn't it wonderful?"

Charlotte smiled and informed me that Sam had also asked her to marry him, but there was no time to buy a ring. Then she delivered the bad news: Sam had received orders to return to his unit in the morning. His leave had been terminated early. She added that James must also report back. We both broke down and cried like babies.

After Charlotte left, I sat on my bed feeling sorry for myself. *It wasn't fair. James and I should have one more full day together before returning to the war.* How quickly and totally the war had passed from my mind during the past several days. I lived completely in the present with no thoughts of the past or immediate future. *The faraway future*, I thought, *would be pure ecstasy. When the war ended, James and I would be living happily ever after, just like in the fairy tales.*

I took a long, warm bath and shampooed my hair. I was thinking about how I would say good-bye. *How hard it was to communicate without words! How could I tell him this had been the happiest week in my entire life, that he was more important than life?* If only I could speak English or he could speak French. I finished dressing and went to James's room. I knocked on the door and he opened it immediately. He looked so handsome in his lieutenant's uniform.

Then my heart sank when I noticed the half-packed duffel bag on his bed. He took me in his arms and we sat down on the end of the bed. He brushed the hair back from my face and kissed me. I wanted so much to tell him what was in my heart, but I had no words. I felt helpless, frustrated by my inability to express my feelings. I could only cling to him and softly sob. Finally, I decided I had cried enough. I sat up, put a smile on my face, and looked at him. We both had tears in our eyes.

"When?" I asked, pointing to his duffel bag.

"Tomorrow," he answered. It was clear he felt as sad as I did.

"I love you, James," I whispered.

"And I love you," he said softly.

It was late and I started toward the door to go back to my room. We would meet again at 6 o'clock in the morning to say good-bye. His train left at 7:45 a.m.

I was unable to sleep that night. I lay awake thinking of James and what the future might hold for us. I vowed to be the perfect wife, keep our home sparkling clean, and always cook his favorite meals. When sleep would not come, I got up and painstakingly wrote him a note using my French-English dictionary.

Finally, I began to doze until my alarm clock went off. I jumped out of bed and dressed carefully for our farewell. Primping before the mirror, I was surprised to find myself looking so rested. I hurried downstairs and found James waiting at the bottom of the stairs. Neither of us was hungry, so we just had coffee and a roll.

When it came time for James to go to the train station, we said good-bye at the hotel. An overnight snowstorm had made transportation scarce and he didn't want me to go to the station with him. I really don't think either of us wanted to face the trauma of another good-bye. He left in a taxi with another serviceman, blowing me a kiss as the taxi departed.

Suddenly, I felt totally exhausted. I found a seat in the lobby, sat down, and was looking aimlessly out the window when Charlotte came in and joined me. She knew by my face and mood that James had left. Sam had left earlier that morning. She had not gone to the station either because it would have made parting harder for both of them.

"Do you really love each other?" I asked Charlotte.

She replied, "Oh, yes. We are going to be married after the war and move to Texas."

I told her they were lucky to have known each other's language; even a little helped so much. "James and I shall marry also, but there were so many things we could not say to each other."

Charlotte remarked that I apparently had not done too badly with the language because James certainly fell in love with me. "He told Sam you were the most beautiful and sweetest girl in the world."

Charlotte changed the subject by telling me she had some very good news. Her request for a transfer to my unit had been approved and we would be working together on the front. I was so elated I jumped up and embraced her. We were both extremely tired, physically and emotionally, so we decided to take a nap before lunch. We agreed to meet in the downstairs dining room at 2 o'clock.

The rest of the day went very quickly and before we knew it, we were on the train and on our way back to the front.

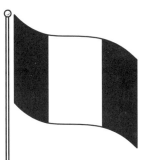

. . . My unit was proud to be a part of the first battalions to enter Germany as we moved toward Karlsruhe. We were finally driving the Boche back into their own country, but it was not easy. . . .

Chapter 13

RETURNING TO THE FRONT was like entering a new world — a world of pain and sadness that I had completely managed to forget during my holiday. I felt buoyant and relaxed and everyone I saw appeared to have a smile for me. The reason for my happiness was perfectly clear: the most wonderful man in the world wanted to marry me. James proved this by writing me every day.

When mail call came, I placed his letters in my pocket until I had a quiet moment and found a place where I could read them in private. Fortunately, I could read some English, even though I could not speak the language. I glowed with happiness after reading his letters; they gave me boundless energy and joy. *I was the luckiest girl in the world.*

Now that Charlotte and I were in the same unit, she tutored me in English and my command of the language improved rapidly. As I composed my daily letters to James, I pronounced the words to myself. *How surprised James will be to discover my proficiency when we would meet again!*

I returned to ambulance duty, only this time as a driver. The young paramedic who served as my partner teased me constantly because I was in love. We worked well together and I actually enjoyed his teasing. I also continued to enjoy my work, and every day my determination to become a professional nurse grew stronger.

In early February 1945 our unit moved into Colmar, in the pocket near the German border, which the Allies had recently liberated. When a brief lull in the fighting temporarily reduced our influx of casualties, we experienced a few hours of unaccustomed free time. The pretty twins, Odette and Lucette, and I set out to explore the old city known for its many beautiful homes.

We were in high spirits as we started out on foot and the weather cooperated with a break in the cold, snowy weather. Odette hopped and skipped on the cobblestone streets of Colmar with exuberance and joy, drawing all the attention of the male population because of her buoyant spirit and bright red hair.

We visited a hat shop, and after trying on different hats, we left and found a perfumery. The proprietor ignored us at first, then reluctantly allowed us to sample a few fragrances. We all enjoyed ourselves immensely, and we returned to our unit that evening happy and refreshed.

The fighting picked up again and our free time quickly came to an end. Our unit moved approximately 20 kilometers outside Colmar and settled in an old house, just as the snow started again. I had not heard from James in several days and began to worry. Charlotte calmed me by telling me that she had not received any letters from Sam either. She convinced me there was no reason to worry, "the mail will soon catch up with us."

Sure enough, five letters from James arrived the next day. He was fine, but had been very busy. He was flying frequent missions into Germany. James seemed confident the war would soon be over. "The Germans were finished," he wrote, "even if they didn't know it yet."

I continued to practice my English every night before going to bed, a ritual I eagerly anticipated. First, I read James's letters, usually several times, savoring every precious word. He usually wrote a few sentences in French, and I often chuckled at his phrasing. Using a dictionary, I laboriously composed my letters, pronouncing the words as I wrote. Then I slept like a baby and often dreamed lovely dreams about the life James and I would share someday.

Charlotte and I met each morning for breakfast and did our best to speak nothing but English. We usually ended up laughing like fools. I discovered that being in love cast a forgiving light on everything.

On the 19th of March, 1945, the First French Army attacked Scheibenhardt, a small village a short distance west of Karlsruhe. After hard fighting the village fell, the first German prize to be captured by the French army. In the words of Commanding General de Tassigny, "The 19th March was a great day for France."[22]

My unit was proud to be a part of the first battalions to enter Germany as we moved toward Karlsruhe. We were finally driving the Boche back into their own country, but it was not easy and we experienced many casualties along the way. The war was not yet over, but everyone sensed the thrill of victory which we knew was very close. It had been nearly five years since the Germans had conquered my country, and now the First French Army was finally reversing the defeats of previous years. Not surprisingly, an urge for revenge spurred on the French soldiers who, with the Allied armies, were now invading Germany.

I thought of Michelle as I drove my ambulance over the Rhine River at Kehl, just east of Strasbourg. I missed her intensely, especially when I entered an ambulance. At times, I could almost feel her presence beside me and I could see her brushing her long hair from her eyes and securing it behind her ears. I would never forget her; war had fused our bond of friendship, first in the Resistance and later in the army.

Fortunately, I had James and he made all that I had endured bearable. The tragedy of my many friends' deaths and my own suffering seemed like a bad dream. The future lay shimmering before me like a sparkling jewel. A few months — at the most — should bring the war to an end and my own life to its bright new beginning.

Germany was now in ruins. There wasn't much left but rubble and shells of buildings. The people seemed disoriented. But my exaltation at entering Germany vanished quickly when I saw the extent of suffering endured by German civilians. Their homes were destroyed, and the quantities of the most essential supplies, including food, were woefully insufficient. We, the French, were occupying Germany just as the Germans had occupied Paris almost five years before.

The French army managed to acquire several undamaged homes just outside Karlsruhe, which enabled us to sleep in real beds. Charlotte, Odette, Lucette, and I were assigned to the home of an elderly German couple, the Schmidts. They welcomed us into their home as "liberators" who were freeing them from their cruel dictator.

Frau Schmidt served us a simple but very tasty dinner. Remembering the shortage of food in Paris, I was almost sure we had severely depleted their small supply. After dinner, we were shown to the bedrooms where we were to sleep. I was led to a small room on the second floor while the three others shared a loft on the third floor.

Just before entering my room, I noticed a large picture of Hitler hanging on the wall. I looked at the brutal dictator with his cruel eyes and arrogant expression. *How could one man*, I pondered, *be responsible for the suffering of millions of people, including the horror in my own life?* I spat on his image, took down the picture and carried it into the small kitchen where Frau Schmidt worked. I waved the picture in front of her and demanded, in broken German, to know why Hitler's picture was displayed in her home.

Frau Schmidt looked at me, then at the picture in dismay as though she was afraid I would hit her. Then she burst into tears. She explained that every German family must have Hitler's picture on display; anyone refusing would be punished by the Gestapo. Something about the expression on her face convinced me she was telling the truth. I walked over and patted her on the shoulder before leaving. I returned to my bedroom and went to bed. The next morning when I went down to breakfast, Hitler's picture was no longer in sight.

The twins were fluent in German, so Odette did most of the talking and translating for all of us. She tried to engage Herr Schmidt in conversation, but he was always so preoccupied she finally gave up. He would talk about nothing but his two sons, who studied at the university.

One day after watching Odette struggling to converse with Herr Schmidt, Frau Schmidt spoke to Odette privately. She explained to Odette how Herr Schmidt had frozen his life in a happier time, when their boys were in school and Germany was honorable and free. She explained that both of their boys had been killed within the same week during the first year of the war. Herr Schmidt had blocked all this from his mind and lived only in the past, before the war had destroyed his family.

After Odette informed us of the situation, we treated our host and hostess with the utmost kindness and sympathy. The Schmidts were good people and made our stay in their home as pleasant as possible.

One day at the hospital, the twins brought in a young Frenchman who looked so much like James I took a special interest in him. He suffered from a nasty thigh wound and frozen legs. When feeling returned to his legs, he suffered excruciating pain, and I spent much of my time with him. After a few days, the pain disappeared but his legs began to swell, and one could detect the sickly, sweet odor that always accompanies gangrene. He understood clearly what the infection meant, and he pleaded with me to prevent the doctors from cutting off his legs. "I want to become a professional entertainer," he told me, "and I cannot live without my legs." His body shook with sobs as I cried along with him.

They took him to surgery the next day and removed both legs. I was with him when he awoke. He looked down at the flat, empty sheets and turned his head toward the wall. He refused to eat and could not sleep without medication. Gradually, he became weaker and after about two weeks, he died. He had simply lost the will to live.

Several days went by without a single letter from James, and I began to worry. Charlotte tried to raise my morale by telling me that he was probably on a mission and could not write, but Sam's letters to her kept coming, and my fears grew each day. I had a hollow feeling in my stomach and my throat felt tight and constricted. As the days passed, I found it difficult to concentrate. When I could, I lost myself in my job where I could forget about James for a short period of time. But I knew something was wrong.

Then one day my Battalion Commander, Colonel Adam, came by to see me and I instinctively knew that James was dead, even before he began speaking. I sat, numbly listening to Colonel Adam's words of sympathy while he told me James had been killed in a mission over Germany. I could neither move nor cry.

I saw that spring was coming. The trees were budding and the sun shone brightly. *How could that be?* My world, my dreams had ended.

I moved around like a zombie the few days after James's death. I took off work, but could neither sleep nor eat. A deep depression totally consumed me. I felt a constant pain, a stricture in my throat through which nothing would pass. I still could not cry.

Colonel Adam came by the Schmidts' house one day to check on me. He tried to cheer me up and urged me to get a good night's sleep and report to work as soon as possible. I finally slept, off and on for a full day, then reported for work. I found it very difficult to face the young soldiers in the hospital. All those fine young men, wounded but alive, reminded me of my loss. I requested a return to ambulance duty, and Dr. Soutille granted my request.

I worked as hard as they would allow and volunteered for all the dangerous missions I could. Work was therapy and when my body was tired, my mind couldn't dwell on anything except the task at hand. And when I was tired enough, I could sleep.

After a week back on the job, Dr. Soutille called me into his office. He was very worried about my depressed state and the methods I was using to hide my grief. Although he realized I had suffered a great loss, he counseled me that pushing myself to the limit and taking unnecessary chances would solve nothing. He looked me directly in the eyes and said firmly, "I think you are trying to get yourself killed. Do you realize how cowardly that is? While you are taking all these noble chances, you are putting other lives in jeopardy as well as your own."

I hung my head, forced to admit to myself that he was right, but I said nothing.

He walked around his desk to my chair, placed his hand on my shoulder, and told me he was going to let me continue working, but he would keep a keen eye on my performance. "If you continue to act irresponsibly," he told me, "I shall have no recourse except to relieve you of your duties."

I stood up, saluted, and left his office.

I went back to work and was careful not to take any unnecessary chances. Dr. Soutille had convinced me that I must act intelligently, and I felt the army was all I had left. A few days later, I received a letter from James's parents, from Minnesota, which Charlotte translated for me. It was a very nice letter expressing their sorrow for my loss as well as their own. They ended the letter by inviting me to visit them at any time and by letting me know I would always be welcome as a member of the family. By the time I finished reading the translation, I was crying. It was the first time I had cried since the news of James's death. Now I just sat and sobbed. The pressure that had built up inside me was released and I began to feel better.

Our love had been wonderful and exciting. Perhaps the happiness that James and I had found with each other balanced the pain I felt. I would always have the memories of our wonderful week together to sustain me in difficult times. With Charlotte's help, I answered the letter from James's parents. I thanked them for their kind letter and promised to visit them if I ever came to the United States; but in my heart I knew I never would. The meeting would be too painful for all of us.

Once again, I put the past behind me and vowed to move forward. This time it would be much harder because the loss of James had almost destroyed my sanity. But gradually, I began to reap the benefits of hard work, and with the passage of time, the grief inside me became more bearable. After several weeks of living in a self-centered world, I began to look around me and realized it was spring. The apple tree outside my window was in full bloom and daffodils and tulips were making their appearances. With the rebirth of nature, I began to feel life flow back into my own body and mind.

I still felt the pain of James's death each day, almost every hour, but occasionally I was able to forget for a moment. I began to smile more and to enjoy conversations with friends.

By May of 1945 the intensity of the fighting had decreased, and we had settled down into a lazy routine at the hospital. On the morning of May 8th, I awoke to the gentle sound of rain on the roof. I felt good because I had slept well that night. The early morning shower had stopped by the time Charlotte and I walked to the hospital. Charlotte remarked that it was good to see me smiling again. The hospital work was slow that morning, and I took my time with my patients.

Suddenly the church bells in Karlsruhe began to ring. At first, no one knew what was happening. Then Charlotte came running in screaming and jumping up and down, almost hysterical with excitement. "Germany has surrendered unconditionally to the Allies. The war is over!" she shouted at the top of her voice.

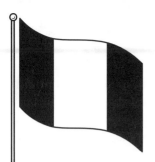

. . . After the euphoria of war's end had passed, work became routine. . . . We began to hear horrible stories about mass exterminations of the Jewish people, stories of people starved, worked to death, and subjected to medical experiments. . . .

Chapter 14

*T*HE WAR WAS OVER! I laughed and danced around the room kissing anyone near me. Everyone was happy that the horror had finally ended. The church bells continued to ring and everyone in Karlsruhe reacted to the news in their own way. Some laughed and danced, others cried, and some just sat staring blankly into space as though a nightmare, too horrible to contemplate, was over.

When Charlotte and I went home that evening, the Schmidts met us with hugs and kisses. Most Germans seemed just as happy as the Allies. They had realized for months Germany was fighting a losing battle. Finally, the devastation and killing would stop and people could concentrate their efforts on rebuilding their cities and lives again.

Charlotte talked me into going to Strasbourg the next day. Lucette went along but Odette was on duty and could not accompany us. The pretty French town was delirious with joy. Everyone was celebrating. The church bells rang and the citizens were euphoric. Drinking and dancing was the order of the day. Strasbourg pulsed with happiness as everyone joined in the festivities.

Pretty Lucette danced through the day. She seemed to draw the young men to her with her beauty and shyness. Toward evening, a young French soldier attached himself to her and would not go away. Charlotte and I sat at a table watching Lucette and Lieutenant Boyer dance in the street, which had been roped off for the occasion.

Soldiers kept coming up to us, repeatedly asking us to dance, but I told Charlotte I didn't feel like dancing. I sat and enjoyed watching the others. Charlotte never left me for very long and was always checking on me.

Eventually, a familiar-looking young man approached my table, but I could not quite place him. He looked at me and asked, "Lisette, is it really you? It's me: Alex."

I immediately hugged him. He looked different, but I could tell that he was indeed Alex. I learned then that his real name was Alexander DuPre. Despite all the time we had spent together in the Resistance, I had known him only as Alex. He had married his Anna and she was pregnant with twins. We filled in the past, since we had last seen each other, and I also learned that he was working as an apprentice in his grandfather's pharmacy shop.

When Charlotte returned to the table, we all decided to find something to eat, and Alex led us to a little out-of-the-way café, jammed with happy, animated people. Alex found the owner and whispered something in his ear, pointing to our small group. The owner smiled and nodded. Alex came back and told us that it would only be a moment before we were seated. The waiter beckoned to us and we were escorted to a room in the back. It was a storeroom with stacks of boxes, but there was a table in the center and the waiter brought several candles for light. Charlotte nudged me: "It's always nice to know someone with connections."

Alex could not stay to have dinner with us — and as he leaned down and kissed me on the cheek he told me, "Have a good life, little Lisette. I will think of you often."

The waiter brought us a superb dinner, and we talked and laughed. We all went dancing and the celebration lasted all night. By sunrise everyone was exhausted. After breakfast, the time had come to return to Karlsruhe. Lucette did not want to leave Henri, but we climbed into the truck and headed back. Charlotte and I were so tired we thought only of sleep, but Lucette was excited and wanted to talk. She wanted us to know all about this wonderful man with whom she had spent the last several hours. Charlotte and I just looked at each other, shrugged, and closed our eyes.

After the euphoria of war's end had passed, work became routine. There were still small pockets of Germans who held out in places, and fighting still occurred, but with increasing rarity.

We began to hear horrible stories about mass exterminations of the Jewish people, stories of people starved, worked to death, and subjected to medical experiments by ghoulish Nazi physicians. In the German concentration camps, the Allied troops found enormous rooms that looked like shower accommodations, but were really gas chambers where prisoners were systematically exterminated. Ovens were found, where bodies had been taken for burning. Estimated deaths were said to be in the millions.

I kept thinking about Victor and Denise, my neighbors in Paris. *What had became of these sweet, gentle people, whose only crime was to have been born Jewish? Had they been in those horrible concentration camps? Had they suffered the unthinkable?* I do not believe that Denise could have survived a place of deprivation, especially after leaving her beautiful baby daughter behind. *And how could Victor have survived without his beloved Denise?* I wished with all my heart that Victor and Denise could have known that I had found little Marie and cared for her. This knowledge, I thought, would have helped to sustain them in whatever ordeals they had to face.

I could not bear to think about it, but their faces haunted me, coming into my mind at unexpected times. I knew I was in danger of slipping into a pit of depression and that I had to do something to save myself. So in my mind, I placed Victor and Denise in heaven, laughing and happy, far away from the ugliness of the world, looking down and guarding their precious daughter.

I kept as busy as possible, but the work had become routine, even boring. The hospital at Karlsruhe was becoming just that — a hospital for sick people and emergencies, no longer a part of a greater cause.

I watched the romance grow between Lucette and Henri Boyer. It seemed that romances had broken out all over. Charlotte received a ring from Sam and they began making plans for a wedding. And Odette was seeing a doctor from the hospital. It made me feel even more alone and I missed James more than ever. I wondered if the deep ache inside me would ever go away.

Henri convinced Lucette that she should put in for a transfer to Freiburg, where he was stationed, and we were all ready for a change by this time, though we wanted to stay together. Odette had broken up with her doctor, so we all applied for transfers. Sam also was stationed near Freiburg, which would make the drive to see Charlotte easier. And so we decided to see Dr. Soutille, who was not surprised at our request. Work had slowed at the hospital and the Freiburg facility needed more help. Our transfers were approved.

Frau Schmidt cried when she heard the news of our departure. "You've been like my own daughters," she said. "Just like the girls I had hoped my sons would marry one day." We had lived with the Schmidts for three months and had become very fond of them. And as Frau Schmidt had shared stories of her life and how the war had destroyed her family, my anger toward her and my hatred of the Germans subsided. I would never forget her kindness to me after James had been killed.

When we arrived at Freiburg, we were separated because there was no home available for the four of us. Charlotte and I were in one home and the twins in another. Charlotte and I were housed with a family of women consisting of a grandmother, daughter, and granddaughter. The grandmother was a stingy, unhappy woman in her late sixties, and she was extremely hostile toward both of us. "You are from France — dirty country, dirty people," she would tell us. The whole family was sullen, aloof, and generally unpleasant. They were determined to blame all their problems on the occupation forces.

The work at the hospital in Freiburg was only tolerable. Again, I was assigned duties as an ambulance driver. Charlotte and Felix, a paramedic, were part of my team. We found out quickly why the hospital was shorthanded. The medical unit was supervised by an unhappy, surly, young captain. He constantly tried to place blame for everything that went wrong on anyone other than himself. In addition, Odette discovered that he was taking drugs that were intended for patients.

When we confronted him with our knowledge, he was furious; he picked up a metal instrument and hurled it through a glass wall, barely missing me. Then, he grabbed my arm, in a frenzy, but fortunately, Lucette came up behind him and hit him over the head with a bedpan. As we dashed out the door and went to find help, we heard glass breaking and crazed laughter. Felix, the paramedic, was standing by the ambulance reading the morning newspaper. I grabbed his arm and told him that he must hurry because the captain had gone crazy and was destroying the hospital. Felix flung his paper aside and told us to stay outside until he called for us. Eventually, we were able to give the man an injection of a sedative to calm him. He had been kneeling on the floor, rocking back and forth, and crying uncontrollably. Once we had plunged the needle into his arm, however, he sank to the floor.

After an investigation in the evening's turmoil, the Freiburg facility was closed temporarily and we were all sent to the hospital at Rottweil near the Black Forest. I was designated to work in surgery with Charlotte and to drive an ambulance on alternate weeks. I liked Rottweil. It not only had natural beauty, but the war had left it almost untouched. The people of Rottweil generally received us nicely, although some Germans showed antagonism toward the French occupation.

The army requisitioned a two-story house for us and the *ambulancieres*. It was very comfortable, and for the first time we were guarded by the Mamadou from Senegal. These large black men were kind, loyal, respectful, and excellent guards. We felt very safe with them.

Henri made the trip to Rottweil at least once a week to see Lucette, and in about the middle of August, he asked her to marry him. They planned their wedding for Christmas.

It was a happy time for all of us.

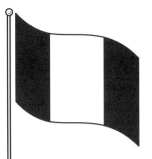

. . . I asked Charlotte how they had died. Charlotte did not want to tell. . . . They had been raped, tortured, and shot.

Chapter 15

WE SETTLED INTO A ROUTINE AT ROTTWEIL, and I enjoyed my work, especially working with Charlotte. The hospital was small, but larger than the one at Freiburg. It provided services for soldiers within about a 160-kilometer radius. Our soldiers were frequently attacked by those Germans who resented the occupation forces, and thus all precautions were taken to guard our troops, including a 10 o'clock curfew and strict warnings to avoid certain areas where a potential for violence existed.

I continued to serve as the ambulance driver and Odette worked as the nurse. We really enjoyed each other's company. Odette was so lively, bright, and lovely, and her flaming red hair never failed to draw attention. She enjoyed the spotlight and always seemed to get into trouble, sometimes getting me involved as well. We would go out after curfew to party, and often we had to sneak back into quarters to avoid getting caught. Life was never dull around Odette.

But in early September, I began to feel unnaturally tired. When I suffered headaches and fever, Charlotte forced me to see Dr. Dupond, who diagnosed my illness as influenza. He told me to go home and directly to bed. I had been assigned to drive the ambulance that day to pick up some patients about 80 kilometers away, but Lucette volunteered to go in my place and dropped in to say good-bye before leaving. Fortunately, I did not spoil any of her plans because Henri was also on duty that night. About 9 o'clock, Lucette, Odette, and Felix, the paramedic, left in the ambulance for the routine trip.

Although feverish, I slept well that night. I was awakened early the next morning by voices outside my door. One of the voices, I thought, belonged to Lucette, and I asked her to come in and talk to me. Instead of Lucette, however, it was Charlotte who poked in her head. She told me the ambulance had not yet returned, and although it was unlikely anything serious had happened, she and some other members of the staff were going to look for them. "They probably had engine trouble and were unable to find help," Charlotte added.

I tried to get up. I wanted to go with her to help find the twins, but Charlotte would not let me.

"We'll be back before you know it," she said.

I couldn't sleep after Charlotte left. I remembered that Henri was coming to see Lucette at 10 o'clock, so I got up and dressed. Still weak and a little dizzy, I managed to walk downstairs to meet Henri. Sure enough, Henri arrived promptly. He was visibly worried when he heard that Lucette had been delayed. I tried to keep him occupied with conversation, but I noticed that he kept looking at his watch as we talked. I did my best to reassure him, but I was too worried myself to be effective. When Henri noticed I was ill, he told me that I should go back to bed. But until I learned what happened, I knew I wouldn't sleep.

Henri abandoned all pretense of calmness as the hours passed. He paced the floor and smoked one cigarette after another. The smoke made me feel more nauseated, so I decided to go outside for some fresh air. But when I stood up, I swayed and nearly fell, just managing to catch myself on the arm of the chair. Henri saw me and took my arm, at the same time insisting I go to bed. He helped me to my room, where I dropped onto my cot and immediately fell into a troubled, exhausted sleep.

When I awoke, it was dark. Again I heard voices outside my door; then Charlotte came into my room. I asked her to turn on the light. There was a hesitation before the light came on and immediately I understood why. Charlotte looked awful. Her face was pale and blotchy and her clothes and hair a mess. She had been crying and when she looked at me, tears began running down her cheeks.

I screamed, "Oh, no!"

Charlotte started sobbing as she came over to me and tried to hold me.

I pushed her away while asking, "How? Was it an accident?"

Charlotte shook her head and told me that the twins had been ambushed. Felix was found first; he had been shot several times and lay just outside the ambulance. There were four dead in the ambulance, obviously the wounded that were being transferred back to Rottweil. At first, they could not find the twins. But while searching the surrounding area, Yves found them in a drainage ditch several yards from the vehicle. They were dead. Charlotte swallowed hard and wiped away her tears with the back of her hand.

I asked Charlotte how they had died. Charlotte did not want to tell me but I insisted. They had been raped, tortured, and shot.

After a moment of silence, I calmly said, "It should have been me. I'm the one who should have died."

Charlotte tried to tell me it was not my fault. "It is no one's fault!" She tried to pull me into her arms, but I turned away from her, refusing to be touched.

"Please go away," I told Charlotte and several others who had stepped into the room. Charlotte pleaded with me to let her stay, but I told her that I needed to be alone for awhile and I was very tired. I sank back against my pillow and closed my eyes. They all left except Charlotte, who lingered behind long enough to tell me she would be right next door if I needed anything.

I just lay there, numb with grief and guilt. I thought about the pain and humiliation Lucette and Odette must have felt as they endured the torture and terror. *I would have happily traded places with Lucette. I would be dead now, free from pain, and in the arms of my beloved James.*

I should have done something more to warn Charles, to prevent them from being shot by the Germans. And Michelle might still be alive if I had helped guide the ambulance that wintry night. And James, dear sweet

James, if he hadn't fallen in love with me, he might still be alive. If, if, if. . . .

My tortured mind kept going over and over the past and each time it came back to the same question. *Why was I still living while all my friends were dead?*

Occasionally, I would drift into an uneasy sleep, only to be awakened again by images of beautiful Lucette with her cloud of red hair, looking adoringly into the face of Henri. The next few days went by in a blur. I was aware of Charlotte and others bringing me food, taking my temperature, and giving me medication. Charlotte did everything possible to help me out of my depressed state; several times a day she came to my room and forced me to bathe, take my medicine, eat, and drink. I found it easier to comply with her wishes than to confront her. What I wanted more than anything else was to be left alone.

My fever finally abated, but I found no reason to leave my bed. I wanted to die. I saw no reason to go on living. Life was such pain — nothing but sadness and sorrow.

Charlotte brought Dr. Dupond to see me. I sat up in bed, smiled meekly, and told him I felt better, but couldn't sleep. He checked me over, noting my fever was gone and the lymph nodes in my neck were smaller, and then gave me three sleeping tablets. He told me to get out of bed several times a day and walk in the garden. "By the end of the week, you should be ready to return to work."

Instead of taking the sleeping pills, however, I wrapped them carefully in a handkerchief and hid them in the back of my dresser. I became a master of deceit. I did everything exactly as requested. I walked in the garden, ate better, and smiled appropriately when talking with friends. But, inside I felt dead.

As expected, I went back to work, and Dr. Dupond and the rest of the staff greeted me enthusiastically. Dr. Dupond informed me that I looked much better although I still had dark circles around my eyes. When I told him I still could not sleep, he gave me another five sleeping pills. I carefully put these pills with the others when I returned to my room. Because I worked in the clinic, I was able to pilfer sleeping pills, one at a time, without being detected. If a patient required several, I would keep one. *After all, the pharmacy could make a mistake and usually the patient didn't even notice.* Occasionally, when a patient scheduled to receive a pill was already asleep, I simply pocketed it.

Charlotte watched over me closely and tried to help me recover, but I turned her away. When Sam came to visit Charlotte, they took me out to dinner. I managed to make polite conversation and pushed my food around on my plate.

It didn't even hurt to see them together because I felt empty, detached, devoid of feelings, as if I was observing the world from another place. The anger that had sustained me through German torture, the pride I felt of being part of my country's liberation, the guilt I harbored about leaving Maman and Suzanne, the faith that God had a purpose for my survival were gone. Nothing touched me. I was just so very tired.

Life must be endured, but only for a little while longer. I approached Dr. Dupond again. *After all, it had been two weeks since he had given me the five pills.* Without the slightest hesitation, he gave me seven more pills.

The time had come. The thought that my pain would soon be over gave me a sense of happiness and relief I had not felt for a long time. That evening Charlotte came into my room before beginning her duty on the night shift. She was delighted to see me smiling and feeling better. I told her that I was fine and she need not worry about me any longer. As she prepared to leave, I thanked her for being such a good friend and gave her a big hug.

Then I went around to pay a small visit to my friends. They all commented on how well I looked and how good it was that I had regained my optimistic outlook. I spoke to my favorite guard, a large black man I called "Pierre Mamadou."

I returned to my room and wrote letters to Grandmere and Grandpere and Maman and Suzanne. It was after midnight when I finished the letters. I put on my prettiest nightgown and took two pills. *Soon, all my suffering will be over.* I grew sleepy, then spilled the rest of the sleeping pills on top of the bed and took them all, two at a time, and closed my eyes. *Soon, I will be with James.*

Suddenly, I remembered Charlotte. I hadn't written Charlotte. It seemed terribly important for me to write to Charlotte, my best friend. I got out of bed and went to the dresser to get pen and paper. But, I felt so dizzy. The bed seemed far away. I fell on the floor before reaching the bed but it was alright. I felt happy as the darkness descended. Charlotte would understand. She would forgive me.

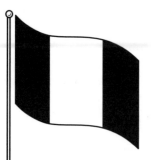

... I did not want to live any longer in a world where good, decent people die so cruelly. . . . Life was too fragile and everyone I loved died. I felt bitter, angry, and cheated.

Chapter 16

I WAS FLOATING PEACEFULLY in the dark as if something was drawing me toward a welcoming light. I felt peaceful, so peaceful. Then I felt someone pulling me, holding me back. I wanted so much to go forward toward the bright, welcoming light but something blocked me. I was jolted. Then someone hit me in the face.

I felt movement, very fast movement. Something cold and hard was thrust down my throat causing me to gag. A harsh light shone in my face and I could not get my hand up to block the glare. But nothing really mattered and once more I sank into darkness. When I awoke, the light hurt my eyes.

Then I remembered. *Oh, no! Why am I still alive?* I tried to put my hands to my eyes to shield them but I couldn't move my hand. I looked down and saw an intravenous drip entering the vein in my arm, strapped to a board so that my elbow couldn't move.

I saw Charlotte looking at me. "Lisette, thank God you're finally awake." She was holding my other hand.

I tried to explain to her that I had wanted to say good-bye, but I felt too exhausted to talk. All I wanted to do was sleep. When I woke again, it was nighttime. A small light illuminated the stark hospital room, and Charlotte sat in a chair beside the window, asleep, snoring lightly. I felt thirsty but there was no water by my bed. I tried to get up and a wave of dizziness and nausea swept over me.

Charlotte suddenly awoke and immediately came over to my bed. "Well, little sister. It's about time you woke up," she remarked.

I asked her for some water. My throat was sore and my head pounded painfully.

Charlotte raised my bed and gave me a sip, warning me to go easy because too much would make me sick.

"What happened?" I asked. "I thought I had it all planned so no one could interfere."

Charlotte replied, "I found you, thank God."

Knowing she worked nights, I asked her how.

Charlotte had felt ill that evening and came home early. "I wouldn't have looked in on you, but your light was on, so I poked my head in. You were unconscious on the floor."

I turned my head away and drew a deep breath. Then I looked at her with displeasure in my eyes. "It would have been so much better if you had just let me die."

Charlotte spoke softly, "I know you feel that way now, but later you will feel differently."

I realized that she did not understand the way I felt. I did not want to live any longer in a world where good, decent people die so cruelly.

"You still have Sam," I told her, "and Lucette isn't dead because of you."

Charlotte quickly responded that I could not blame myself for the death of Lucette or anyone else. "That is in the hands of God, not you."

"Just go away and leave me alone," I replied sharply.

Charlotte backed out the door with tears streaming down her face, but not before informing me that no matter what I said, she would be back soon.

Friends were in and out of my room every few minutes for the next several days. I treated them all alike, remaining very cold and distant. I was too busy feeling sorry for myself to return their kindness. I resolved never to let anyone get close to me again. *Life was too fragile and everyone I loved died.* I felt bitter, angry, and cheated.

One morning I looked up as a visitor entered my room, and to my surprise, it was Henri Boyer. His hair was neatly combed and his clothes were immaculate as usual, but his eyes were red and his face haggard. I burst into tears when I recognized him. Tears were also streaming down his face as he sat down on my bed and took me in his arms. We both cried while he held me and I tried to explain how sorry I was about what had happened.

"I know," he said, "we are all sorry; but you must not blame yourself. Lucette was just doing her job." Henri had spent a lot of time with Lucette's parents, and they were also having a hard time accepting the loss of their daughters. He told me that both Lucette and Odette had talked and written about how much they loved and admired me.

"If the situation have been reversed," Henri continued, "you would have filled in for Lucette, or anyone else who was ill, without a second thought. Lisette, you must get it through your head that no one blames you but yourself. You must go on and try to make the best of your life, because that is what Lucette and James would have wanted you to do."

For the first time since Lucette and Odette had died, I wanted to reach out to another human being. I knew Henri understood how I felt, because he had lost someone dear, just as I had lost James.

Before leaving, Henri asked me to promise him that I would not give up on life again. I hesitated a long time before telling him that I would try. Henri reached over, kissed me on the cheek, and said Lucette loved me dearly and would have been disappointed if her death made me give up on life.

That evening Charlotte came by with a bouquet of lovely fall flowers. She pulled up a chair to my bedside and told me, "Although I know you do not want me here, I have some things I want to talk about."

I replied that I really did not need a lecture, and promised not to try and take my life again, if that was her concern.

She continued by telling me how she had always admired my spirit and courage. I was the one person she believed capable of absorbing the adversities of life and still remain strong and emotionally stable.

I replied angrily: "I don't want to hear that. If you have nothing else to say you should leave."

Charlotte's eyes flashed. "You will listen to me," she said. "You are my best friend and that gives me the right."

"I don't want you to be my friend!" I shouted back. "Everyone who cares for me dies."

"Is that what you really think, Lisette? All of your friends died while serving their country, as you have done day after day. It is not because of you they died, but for France."

Great sobs shook my whole body.

"Don't you see?" Charlotte continued. "You have to live and learn to be happy or all those who have died before will have died in vain."

I asked her how I could go on when life seemed so futile, so empty.

"Come with me. We'll walk in the garden and maybe I can show you," she said.

I put on my robe and followed Charlotte through the hospital corridors into the small enclosure. A breeze carried an autumn chill in the air as a glorious sunset was in progress. The tiny formal garden was fragrant with fall flowers — marguerites and asters. Charlotte led me to a small bench and we sat down together. We watched the sunset in silence.

Charlotte then reminded me of how beautiful the world was, how God had fashioned these wonderful colors for us to enjoy. I told her that God had also made men who committed barbarous atrocities to other men and permitted war that was ugly and evil.

"But, it's over Lisette. The war is over. Just as we are beginning to rebuild our cities, you must begin to rebuild your life."

We continued talking in the garden for another hour before returning to our rooms.

I slept very well that night, without dreams or nightmares. When Dr. Dupond came by to see me the following day, I was dressed and ready to leave the hospital. I cheerfully told him that I was feeling fine and would like to return to work.

He motioned for me to sit down; he wished to talk to me. Despite the very difficult time I had been through, Dr. Dupond warned, I would continue to have bouts of despair. He wanted to be certain I was well before I left the hospital.

I listened to Dr. Dupond, but still insisted on leaving.

He finally agreed to release me provided I promised to eat more, get plenty of rest, and spend more time in the sun. Also, I must come into the hospital every day to allow him to check my progress. I agreed to these conditions, and Dr. Dupond approved my release.

I was true to my word, and on the third day Dr. Dupond told me the commanding officer had agreed with him that I needed a furlough. He advised me to take a real vacation — to go home and see my family; he did not want to see my face for an entire month. By the time I arrived back at the house where we were quartered, I was determined to go and see Maman and Suzanne.

Even the letter waiting for me was not enough to change my mind. It was from Odette and Lucette's parents in Joigny. They asked me to attend a memorial service for the twins in two weeks. But first I needed to go to Paris, and this time — home.

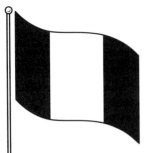

. . . Maman told me that the Gestapo had hounded her for several weeks after I had been whisked away by the Resistance.

Chapter 17

CHARLOTTE KNOCKED ON MY DOOR as I was packing. When she asked what I was doing, I told her about my forthcoming leave to visit Maman and Suzanne. Charlotte was a little surprised. She had been under the impression I had no family since I never spoke of them. I explained how Maman and I had never been close, and that my participation in the Resistance, which she opposed, had made our relationship impossible. I had neither seen nor had contact with Maman for a year and a half.

"She must be desperately worried about you," Charlotte remarked.

"I am not sure she cares one way or the other," I replied. "She never seemed to want me around as a child."

Charlotte chuckled and said her mother was much the same; mothers were just that way. Charlotte offered to go with me to Paris, but I knew this was something I needed to do alone.

It was a rare, beautiful October day in 1945 — crisp, cool, and bright — when I left for Paris. I said good-bye to my friends and boarded the truck for Strasbourg where I caught the Paris train. After boarding, I took a short nap.

When I woke up, a woman was sitting next to me with a three-month-old baby. My thoughts immediately went to Victor and Denise and I wondered how little Marie was doing. *She would be almost three years old!* I remembered how happy Maman had been when Marie lived with us. She brought out Maman's tender side, a side that I seldom had the opportunity to observe. I would ask Maman where Marie lived and perhaps try to visit her.

I arrived in Versailles the next morning and checked into a hotel. If Maman was still angry, I wanted to have a place to stay. I was so tired that after checking in I ate a light lunch and tried to nap. I could not sleep, so I thought about James. I was horrified when I was unable to remember what he looked like. *How odd!* I took the only photograph I had of him and looked at it closely, but it did not seem to help much. He was standing by his airplane, grinning, but his features were not distinct. I rolled over and went to sleep.

I woke up around 2 o'clock, in plenty of time to take the train into Paris. I packed a small valise with a toothbrush and a change of underwear and boarded the train. On the way I rehearsed what I was going to say to Maman, and before I knew it, I had arrived at my destination.

Our apartment was only about three blocks from the metro and it felt good to walk. The beautiful day was turning cold and a strong wind had come up. I was both looking forward to seeing Maman and Suzanne and afraid that the reunion might not go very well. I walked one more block and could see their window. It was closed and the shades were up. A feeling of apprehension came over me, but I kept walking. I still felt wounded and vulnerable.

Nothing seemed to have changed since I had left. The courtyard was covered with fallen leaves and the tiny rose garden had a few tired blossoms. I entered the door and saw the same old dirt-colored carpet covering the stairs. I walked up the stairs, stood in front of the apartment door, took a deep breath, and began knocking on the door. The door opened and I saw Suzanne, staring at me blankly. "Suzanne," I said, "it's me, Elisabeth."

Suzanne's eyes widened and she gasped, putting her small hand over her mouth. She looked so bewildered that I started toward her, meaning to reassure her, but she backed away.

"Maman," she called, in a strange strangled voice, "please come here."

She made no move to let me into the apartment; we just stood there looking at one another. Maman came into the room and when she saw me, she put her hand over her heart. Then she gasped and promptly fainted.

I knelt beside Maman and she began laughing and crying at the same time. "Elisabeth, is it really you?" she asked. "I thought you were dead. The army told me you were missing in action last year, and when I heard nothing more, I assumed you were dead."

Maman looked at me lovingly and tenderly touched my face. "You are so thin, Elisabeth," she said.

Suzanne came over and shyly hugged me. She had grown up. She seemed tall for her 15 years. She had a beautiful, sweet face with large brown eyes and shiny black hair. I looked at her and said, "Oh, Suzanne, you're beautiful," as I returned her hug.

All misunderstandings were forgiven and we had several wonderful days together. We did not go anywhere, but spent our time reminiscing and catching up with each other's lives. Maman told me that the Gestapo had hounded her for several weeks after I had been whisked away by the Resistance. Finally, Madame la Directorice, my Red Cross director and contact for the Resistance, informed Maman that I was safe.

We all went together to visit Annick's grave and to put on her headstone the autumn flowers that she had loved so much. Maman told me she had ordered a memorial plaque for Papa, but it wasn't in place yet.

I put my arms around Maman's shoulders and told her I wanted to be a nurse "so I can help all the people who needed help, like our dear Annick."

When we arrived back home, Maman sat down beside me and matter-of-factly told me, "Elisabeth, I do not want you to be a nurse."

"I'm grown-up now," I replied, "and I have made up my mind. I already have a grant for my studies and the government will pay all my expenses." I saw the disappointment in Maman's eyes. I explained that I must first earn my baccalaureate degree, then I would go to a fine nursing school located right there in Paris. "You must understand," I told Maman, "I need to be independent and make my own way."

Maman smiled. "You've always been independent, Elisabeth, since you were a toddler. You know I just want the best for you."

On our last evening together, Maman cooked all my favorite foods —

lamb with roasted chestnuts and fried potatoes with peas and small onions. I felt warm and comfortable with Maman for the first time in many years. I decided it was time to tell her about my love for James and his death on a bombing mission.

Maman reacted as I expected. There were no signs of sympathy after she found out James was an American. If we had married, James would have taken me away from her again.

I left Maman's house with a new sense of relief and the knowledge that my relationship with her had changed. At last, I felt loved and respected by Maman, which made me happy and more content with myself than ever before.

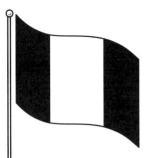

. . . I have always been haunted by the images of the Jewish people I saw slaughtered at the hands of the Nazis. . . . In 1954, . . . people were still afraid to talk about those civilians who were missing — especially suspected Jews and their families.

Epilogue

AFTER THE WAR, my brother, Arthur, was recalled to active duty in the French army. He married, had two children, and died in France in 1989. Suzanne married, had three children (one boy and two girls), and now lives in Aix-en-Provence in southern France.

Maman died from a heart attack in December 1965. She never approved of my career in nursing, and she was very disappointed that I moved to the United States. However, I gained a greater understanding of Maman's attitudes when I learned that she had survived her own horrors in Armenian concentration camps before and after World War I. I can see that although we did not always agree and I did not always understand her motives, in many ways she had tried to protect me.

Grandpere lived to be 102 years old and Grandmere to be 98 years old in the Villeneuve St. Georges stone house, which Grandpere had

Elisabeth, Suzanne, and Maman, *circa* 1954.

Grandmere and Grandpere, *circa* 1930.

built many years earlier. At the age of 100, Grandpere still chased Grandmere around the house, pinching her on her buttocks and proclaiming, "I just could not keep my hands off such a beautiful lady." He was active and alert until the day he died, as was Grandmere.

I saw Alexander DuPre one more time after our chance meeting in Strasbourg. He took the photographs of me receiving the *Croix de Guerre*. To my knowledge, he lived a full and happy life with Anna.

As planned, Charlotte and Sam married after the war, and Charlotte moved to Junction, Texas, with her husband. She and I remained good friends until her death in 1988.

The city of Joigny in France honored the twins, Odette and Lucette Lecocq, by naming a street for them. In February 1997, I was able to visit Joigny and their burial site in Ulm, Germany. Although an investigation was made into their murders, no one was ever arrested for the crime.

I have always been haunted by the images of the Jewish people I saw slaughtered at the hands of the Nazis. On April 30, 1995, I was one of twelve honorees at a candle-lighting service in Oklahoma City commem-

orating *Yom HaShoah* (Holocaust Remembrance). I am very proud to say that in Jerusalem, a tree has been planted in my name, honoring my work in the French Resistance.

In 1995, I submitted the names of Victor and Denise, along with their country of origin, Poland, to a group that traces Jewish families lost during the Holocaust. The search process takes many years, but I hope someday to learn about their fate. In 1954, when I returned to Paris from service in the French army in Vietnam, I searched in earnest for their daughter, Marie. Unfortunately, people were still afraid to talk about those civilians who were missing — especially suspected Jews and their families. To this day, Marie has never been found.

In October 1945, I returned to Germany where I continued to serve in the French occupation forces. Because I wished to return to school, I decided to leave the army to study for my baccalaureate (high school). I returned to Paris where I received my discharge from the French army on March 7, 1946.

Dr. Soutille and Colonel Adam suggested that all members of our Resistance unit meet weekly at Rue de l'Université. We called ourselves the "French Combatants," and I enjoyed spending time with my *Maquisard* friends during peacetime.

In Paris, I again lived with Maman in the apartment as I prepared to resume my schooling. It was at this time I developed a serious medical problem. Both of my knees became infected by the shrapnel from the injuries I had received in the Colmar Pocket.

Surgery at the Tenon Hospital in July 1945 successfully removed the remaining shrapnel, but did not cure the infection. For this I needed penicillin, but it was in short supply, and the hospital authorities informed me

---

Page opposite: On June 10, 1948, at the Hotel des Invalides in Paris, Elisabeth was awarded the *Croix de Guerre* (Cross of War) with bronze star, a very high honor in France. The day after the fire at the Infirmary, in September 1944, Colonel Adam had asked to see her, complimenting her on her courage and fast action. Elisabeth believes that Colonel Adam recommended her for the *Croix de Guerre,* a decoration that was rarely given to army nurses.

In the photo, Alexander DuPre is holding the camera. Directly behind him, standing to the far left, first row, is Ange-Marie Miniconi, "Jean-Marie," for whom Elisabeth's Resistance unit was named. Most of the others in the photograph were also in *Reseau Jean-Marie*. Many of the awards were presented to the next-of-kin because the honoree had given his or her life for France.

RÉPUBLIQUE FRANÇAISE

Guerre 1939-1945

CITATION

DECISION N° 783

LE SECRETAIRE D'ETAT AUX FORCES ARMEES " GUERRE "

CITE   A L'ORDRE DU REGIMENT

K A P E L J A N Elisabeth   -   (F.F.C.)

" Jeune infirmière, ayant un courage remarquable, a servi la cause de la résistance avec une abnégation digne d'éloges. De Mai 1944 à la libération, infirmière du maquis dans l'Yonne, a prodigué ses soins aux blessés et aux malades. A toujours montré même dans les circonstances les plus critiques un dévouement et un mépris du danger hors de pair."

CETTE CITATION COMPORTE L'ATTRIBUTION DE LA CROIX DE GUERRE AVEC ETOILE DE BRONZE, ET ELLE ANNULE ET REMPLACE CELLES ACCORDEES ANTERIEUREMENT POUR LES MEMES FAITS.

FAIT à PARIS, le 15 Juin 1948

Signé : Max LEJEUNE

POUR AMPLIATION
PARIS, le 15 Juin 1948
L'Administrateur de 1° Cl.
BEAULMONT
Chef du Bureau Décorations
P/O. Le Capitaine LAMOTHE

Croix de Guerre citation (783) in French and English (page opposite)

THE FRENCH REPUBLIC

WORLD WAR II 1939-1943
CITATION # 783

The Secretary of the Armed Forces granted by the order of the Regiment to

Kapelian, Elisabeth
F.F.C.
Combatant in the French Forces

A young nurse, displaying remarkable courage, has served the cause of the Resistance with praiseworthy self-sacrifice from May 1944 to the liberation, as a nurse in the Resistance in the Department of Yonne. She has prodigiously tended for the sick and the wounded, always demonstrating even in the most critical circumstances a dedication to duty and a disdain for danger beyond compare.

This honor includes the granting of the Cross of War with Bronze Star and it supersedes all other awards previously granted for the same accomplishments.

Traduit par
Phyllis Laws
30-4-93

Subscribed and sworn to before me this __3__ day of __May__ 19__93__.
My commission expires __4-15-97__.

_____ Notary Public

---

none could be obtained. Desperate for a cure, I took the bold step of writing General de Gaulle, hoping he would use his influence to help a former member of the Resistance. Even before I received General de Gaulle's reply, the hospital obtained the necessary penicillin and I began to recover. Although my stay at Tenon Hospital lasted about three months, and the

FONDATION DE LA FRANCE LIBRE

En 1994, par décret paru au journal officiel portant la date symbolique du 18 juin, la Fondation de la France libre a été créée et reconnue d'utilité publique.

Présidée par le général d'armée Jean Simon, Chancelier de l'Ordre de la Libération, président national de l'Association des Français libres, son conseil d'administration est composé des personnalités des Forces françaises libres suivantes :

PIERRE MESSMER,
ancien Premier ministre, Compagnon de la Libération

JACQUES CHABAN-DELMAS,
ancien Premier ministre, Compagnon de la Libération

JEAN MARIN,
vice-président

YVES EZZANO,
général d'armée aérienne, représentant les Compagnons de la Libération

JEAN MATTEOLI,
ancien ministre, président de la Fondation de la Résistance

BERNARD SAINT HILLIER,
général d'armée, Compagnon de la Libération

EMILE CHALINE,
vice-amiral d'escadre

GEORGES CAÏTUCOLI,
secrétaire général

JACQUES PIGNAUX DE LAROCHE,
trésorier

La puissance publique est représentée par:
Monsieur le minsitre de l'Intérieur
Monsieur le ministre de la Défense
Monsieur le ministre des Anciens Combattants et victimes de guerre
Monsieur le maire de Paris ville compagnon de la libération.

Elisabeth received the Cross of Lorraine for her service in the French Resistance during World War II, presented with the certificate above.

Opposite page: The "Attestation" describing the Resistance unit to which Elisabeth belonged.

SECRÉTARIAT d'ÉTAT aux FORCES ARMÉES
(Guerre)
DIRECTION DU PERSONNEL
MILITAIRE DE L'ARMÉE DE TERRE
6ème BUREAU

ATTESTATION
d'appartenance aux F. F. C.

Original à conserver par l'intéressé.

Aucun duplicata ne pouvant être délivré, le porteur de la présente attestation ne devra sou dépôt, en au circonstance... o de besoin établir des copies conformes. —

N 59971

RÉFÉRENCE : I.M. Nº 407/FFCI/Adm du 17 Avril 1947

Madame **KAPELIAN** Elisabeth

Né le 15/12/24

a servi en qualité d'**AGENT P. 1**

du 1/5/44 au 30/9/44

au réseau JEAN-MARIE BUCKMASTER

~~Grade~~ ~~réel~~

PARIS, le 16 AVRIL 1948

CERTIFIÉ EXACT
Pour le Général, Directeur
Le Lt colonel de DIONNE
chef du B.L. ~~Délégué Général~~ des Forces Françaises Combattantes de l'Intérieur

Les services accomplis en qualité d'"Agent P." comptent comme **services militaires actifs**, suivant les dispositions de l'I. M. citée en référence.

Above: This CNFC (*Confederation Nationale France Combattante*) card was issued to Elisabeth in 1996 by the French government to attest to the fact that she was a member of the French Resistance and a combattante in the French army. Below: The card issued to her in 1948.

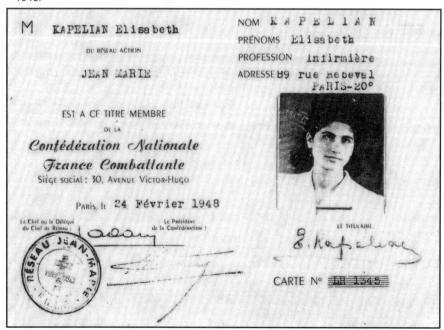

Dr. Soutille with his two children, *circa* 1949.

rehabilitation of my knees took about a year, I still managed to earn my baccalaureate in June 1948.

Between 1948 and 1950, I began and completed my training to become a nurse, thus realizing one of my childhood dreams. On March 24, 1950, I reenlisted in the French army and volunteered for service in Vietnam, where I served as an army nurse from July of 1950 until I returned to Paris in February of 1953. I was awarded the Colonial Medal and the Commemorative Medal of the Campaign of Indochina.

While in Vietnam, I met a lovely couple who shared many photographs and stories about the United States. I returned to France to find no jobs for nurses, so in 1955, I decided to go to the United States and work in a French hospital run by the Sisters of Mercy in New York.

Because I spoke Spanish more fluently than English, I decided to move to El Paso, Texas, where I continued working as a pediatric nurse at Hotel Dieu Hospital and attended the University of Texas at El Paso. There, at Fort Bliss, I met my husband, Robert W. Sevier, a career U.S. Army officer. We were married on July 25, 1958.

Although I loved nursing, the strain of seeing sick children suffer became too great and I was reminded of my hardships during Vietnam. So,

> LE GÉNÉRAL DE GAULLE   COLOMBEY-LES-DEUX-EGLISES, le 20 JUILLET 1946
>
> Mademoiselle,
>
> J'ai pris connaissance avec attention de la lettre que vous m'avez adressée.
>
> Vous ne manquerez pas d'être tenue informée de la suite qui aura pu être réservée à votre requête.
>
> Veuillez agréer, Mademoiselle, l'assurance de mes sentiments respectueux.
>
> *[signature]*
>
> Mademoiselle Lisette KAPELIAN
> Salon Richard Wallace
> Hopital Tenon
> PARIS (20 ème)

The French (above) and English (page opposite) versions of General Charles De Gaulle's reply to Elisabeth's request for penicillin.

in 1964, while my husband was serving an unaccompanied tour in Free China (Formosa), I decided to pursue another career. As Maman had wished, I graduated from the New Mexico State University in May of 1971 (with highest honors) with a degree in education.

Bob and I were blessed with four beautiful children — all of whom are now happy and successful adults. We also had the privilege of hosting four foreign exchange students — two from France, one from Germany, and one from Belgium. And I continued to enjoy young people by teaching

> General De Gaulle   COLOMBEY-LES-DEUX-EGLISES, 20 JULY 1945
>
> Madmoiselle,
>
> I have carefully considered the letter which you sent me.
>
> I shall not fail to keep you informed of the outcome of the request which you sent me.
>
> Please accept, Mademoiselle, my most respectful sentiments.
>
> Signature
>
> Mademoiselle Lisette KAPELIAN
> Salon Richard Wallace   Translated by: Phyllis Laws
> Hospital Tenon
> Paris (20 eme)
>
> Subscribed and sworn to before me this 22 day of Sept 1993.
> My commission expires April 15, 1997.
>
> Kathryn R. Anderson, Notary Public

them, first in El Paso, until 1975, and later in Edmond, Oklahoma, until my retirement in 1997.

My students were instrumental in convincing me to write this book. The memories from my life as a *Maquisard* are bitter-sweet and many of the horrors I did not want to recall, let alone retell. However, with their support, and the encouragement of my husband and our friend Dr. Richard Peters, I was able to recount many of the events of my teenage years in the Resistance. My hope is that in writing this work, I have brought honor to the memories of my many friends in the *Maquis*.

Name and first name: KATELIAN, Elisabeth.
(born the 12.15.1924 in Larissa (Greece))

Serial Number: 45-758-08046.

DETAILS OF SERVICES AND TRANSFERS

Services and transfers	Date	References
Enlisted voluntarily for the duration of the war at the induction center of Belfort with the title of UA 8 the	2.21.45	Enlistment confirmed
Assigned to the infirmary AFAT the	2.21.45	9/ 1762
Transferred to the military Post Office.	2.21.45	AM n°5172 on the 2.24.45
Transferred to the 32nd UA in Paris with the intention of obtaining her discharge.		AM 5381 on the 2.1.46
Discharged by the 32nd UA the	3.7.46	Slip n°754
Reenlisted for two years at the induction center of Paris with the title of C.E.F.E.O.	3.24.50	Enlistment confirmed S/n°119
Assigned to the C.R.P.F.I. of Margival the	3.24.50	
Transferred to the military hospital D. Larrey in Versailles.		
Classified 5th category alc	3.24.50	D.7894/RA
Assigned to the S.I.C.I. Indochina with the title of nurse's aid.	8.11.50	AM 1520 8.11.50
Left Paris the	8.17.50	
Landed in Saigon the	8.20.50	
Was appointed to the service of Dr. Colonel DSS PFUS hlc	8.22.50	AM 6996/ DSS/1
Assigned DAIC/FVS, chief of Saint Jacques		AM 2140
Promoted 5th category 2nd Grade alc	12.15.50	8.24.50
Promoted 5th category 3rd Grade hlc	6.15.51	D.79 5.25.50
Assigned to the DAIC 4 TCV at the service of the Dr. Colonel, director of health services of the land forces of the Vietman Center.		AM 3523 DSS 7.10.51
Arrived at the unit and admitted there	7.20.51	
Assigned A.C.M. 507		AM 2989. 7.20.50
Assigned to the infirmary of the garrison of Tourane		AM 1543/SCA 4.8.52
Given permission to stay two more years in Indochina		D.1897/BSS 4.30.52
Promoted to the 4th category alc	1.1.52	D.86- 5.9.52
Reenlisted for six months with the title of DAIC/CV at the military post of Tourane.	3.24.52	Enlistment confirmed S/ 515 D.22281
Given permission to extend her stay in CC for six months alc	8.20.52	7.13.52

Subscribed before me this 10th day of February, 1965.

Notary Public
My Commission Expires November 7, 1968

Transmitted and certified conform to the original

Christiane M. Shops.

Above and opposite: Elisabeth's military records.

SERVICE RECORDS (CONTINUED)

Name: KAPELIAN
First Name: Elisabeth
Divorced: Forin
Married Name: SEVIER

Serial Number: 45-758-08046

Campaigns			Citations and Rewards	Decorations
from the	to the	against		
5.1.44	9.30.44	CD PVC	Cited to the order of the regiment (n°783 on the 6.10.48) "Young nurse with remarkable courage, served, from May 1944 until the liberation, the cause of the resistance with an abnegation worthy of praise. Was a nurse in the Maquis of Etang Neuf (Yonne). Devoted herself to the care of the wounded and sick" A	Commemorative Medal 39-45 pin EV
2.21.45	5.8.45	QD army		Bronze Croix de Guerre.
8.17.50	8.20.50	1/2 s Air		Colonial Medal, pin EO
8.21.50	2.24.53	QD EO		(Patent n°304510) on the 7.10.51.
2.25.53	3.23.53	1/2 c sea		
3.24.53	7.17.53	CD CFC		Commemorative Medal of the campaign of Indochina.
			Has always shown even in the most dangerous conditions, outstanding courage. This citation includes the Croix de Guerre in bronze.	

Translated conformed to the original
Christiane M Shoop

Subscribed before me this 10th day of February, 1965

Margaret Peabody
Notary Public
My Commission Expires November 7, 1966

```
                    SERVICE RECORDS (CONTINUED)

        1st Region                          Department: Seine

    Name: KAPELIAN                          Serial Number:
    First Name: Elisabeth                   45-758-0 046
    Divorced: Forin
    Married Name: SEVIER,

        DETAILS OF SERVICES AND TRANSFERS: (Continued)
```

Services and Tranfers	Date	References
Reenlisted for six months with the title of DALC/CV at the hlc military Post of Tourane as a nurse	9.24.52	Enlistment paper S/n° 740 Am 239/DSS
Transfered to the SICX Indochina (RPA) Repatriated for the rest of the duration of the enlistment	2.10.53	on the 2.3.53.
Embarked on the S.S. KERGUELEN the	2.25.53	
Landed in Marseille the	3.23.53	
On furlough from the 3.24 to the	7.17.53	
Attached to the C.E.M.T.C. hlc	2.25.53	
Discharged the	7.18.53	as a nurse.

* Declared her intention to live
in Verdun, 15 rue de la Division
Blindee USA to serve as a agent P1   *1 has served.
from the 5.1. 1944 to the 9.30.1944.
in the network of Jean Marie Buckmaster
of the French fighting forces.
(Attestation FFC n° 59,971 on the 1.27.49.

```
              Certified conforme to the
              original.
              Commandant of the Recruting Center.
              26 August 1961.
        Subscribed before me this 10th day of February, 1965.

                                    _____
                                          Notary Public
                                    My Commission Expires November 7, 1966

    Translated and certified conforme to the original.
                            Christiane Shop
```

More of Elisabeth's military records.

Certificate of demobilization from military service, issued March 7, 1946.

FICHE DE DÉMOBILISATION

Modèle N° ....
N° de la fiche : 134
N° de l'exemplaire : I

Organe démobilisateur : U.A. 32. AFAT Paris

1. NOM : (en lettres majuscules d'imprimerie) APELLIAN Prénoms : Elisabeth
2. Bureau de recrutement : M.A.P.
3. N° Matricule : 11.256
4. Classe de recrutement : 44
5. Classe de rattach. : 1 années de service ....
6. Date et lieu de naissance : né le 15.12.2. .... à ....
7. Département : ....
8. Nationalité : français de naissance - naturalisé - recensé art. 3 - Indigène (2) ..........M.I.) (1) Étranger (nationalité) .... pour Paris et Lyon indiquer l'arrondissement
9. Adresse avant les hostilités (2-9-39) Commune .... Rue 89 rue Delessel Département Seine
10. Adresse où se retire l'intéressé Commune Osny, chez M. Boyer Rue Collège Ardaillon Département Algérie
11. Situation de famille (1) Célibataire, marié, veuf divorcé
12. Nombre d'enfants vivants ou ayant vécu simultanément ....
13. Profession principale infirmière
14. Arme .... Subdivision d'arme ....
15. Dernier corps et unité d'affectation U.A.8.

World War II Certificate of Release from the military.

ΔΗΜΑΡΧΟΣ ΛΑΡΙΣΗΣ

MAIRE DE LARISSA

Larissa (Grèce) le 8 novembre 1961.

Madame Elisabeth Sevier
P.O. Box 224
Hecker (Illinois) U.S.A.

Chère Madame,

      Nous avons bien reçu votre estimée sans date concernant votre état civil et nous venons par la présente vous faire connaitre que malgré tous nos efforts pour donner suite à votre demande il nous a été absolument impossible de trouver des traces de votre séjour dans notre ville.
' A part les recherches effectuées sur nos registres d'état civil, nous avons recourru auprès de vos vieux compatriotes demeurant encore à Larissa, mais malheureusement, même ceux-ci n'étaient à même de nous donner une information quelconque sur votre cas, étant donné qu'aucun arménien a été enregistré sur nos livres.

      Nous regrettons donc vivement à cet effet et nous prions d'agréer, chère madame, nos sincères salutations.

LE MAIRE DE LARISSA

Démètre Hadjiyannis.

The letter from the Mayor of Larissa, Greece, responding to Elisabeth Kapelian Sevier's request for information regarding her birth registration. (Translation appears on the next page.)

Mayor of Larissa

Larissa (Greece) 8 November 1961.

Madame Elisabeth Sevier
P.O. Box 224
Hecker (Illinois) U.S.A.

Dear Madame,

We have received your estimate concerning your birth date and we herewith inform you that we have tried everything in order to satisfy your request, but it was impossible to find a trace of your birth in our city.

We have looked everywhere in the registry for your birth certificate and have even called on your mother's friends at Larissa. Unfortunately, they could not give any information because none of the Armenians had been registered in our books.

We regret this and we agree that the records are unavailable, with our sincere regards.

The Mayor of Larissa

Demetre Hadjiyannis.

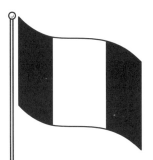

Author's Note

*D*URING THE WAR, my Resistance comrades used pseudonyms, though Dr. Soutille and Colonel Adam used their real names while working with the *Reseau Jean-Marie*. I later learned the name of Alexander DuPre and thus use his real name throughout the text. However, I never learned the real names of the others, including Charles and Michelle.

The dates herein are as accurate as I can remember after the lapse of so many years. There are certain times and events that I recall much better than others, and I have naturally concentrated on what I remember best. I have found it easier to remember what happened than when it happened. Nevertheless, with the help of Dr. Richard Peters and many books, I believe the dates are essentially accurate.

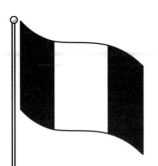

Notes

Introduction

1. Dwight D. Eisenhower, *Crusade in Europe* (Garden City, NY: Doubleday & Company, 1948), 296.
2. Maurice J. Buckmaster, *Specially Employed: The Story of British Aid to French Patriots of the Resistance* (London: The Batchworth Press, 1952), 100.

Prologue

3. There is some uncertainty about the origin of the word, but it appears to have been in use at least as early as 1870. See Douglas L. Buffman, *The New York Times*, April 7, 1916, 10.
4. Robert O. Paxton, *Vichy France: Old Guard and New Order, 1940-1944* (New York: Columbia University Press, 1972), 292-293, 311, 369-70; John F. Sweets, *Choices in Vichy France: The French Under Nazi Occupation* (New York: Oxford University Press, 1994), 24-29, 168, 212; Willis Thornton, *The Liberation of Paris* (New York: Harcourt, Brace & World, Inc., 1962), 46-47.

Chapter 1

5. The German army made no serious attempt to breach the Maginot Line, but sent the main thrust through the mountainous Ardennes sector. Bypassing Paris, the Germans headed for the English Channel, where they entrapped the British and French forces at Dunkirk. The French held high expectations for the Maginot Line as a defense stronghold and the rumors, fears, and false reports rampant in Paris lead to panic and Maman's remark. See Anthony Kemp, *The Maginot Line: Myth and Reality* (New York: Military Heritage Press, 1988), chapters 10 and 11.

Chapter 2

6. For the text of Pétain's speech, see Richard Griffiths, *Pétain: A Biography of Marshal Philippe Pétain of Vichy* (Garden City, NY: Doubleday and Company, 1952), 240.
7. Paul Farmer, *Vichy: Political Dilemma* (New York: Columbia University Press, 1955), chapters 4 and 5.
8. For the text of General de Gaulle's June 18th address made on the BBC, see Charles de Gaulle, *War Memoirs*, Vol. I, *The Call to Honor* (New York: The Viking Press, 1955), 83-84; On June 19, 1940, *Le Petit Provencal* published the address on the front page, and several other papers carried news of the broadcast. See H. R. Kedward, *Resistance in Vichy France: A Study of Ideas and Motivation in the Southern Zone, 1940-1942* (Oxford: Oxford University Press, 1978), 210.
9. After the war, many resistants claimed that they heard de Gaulle's historic speech on June 18th, or later, when the BBC rebroadcast it. They could not have heard it after June 18th, because the speech was not recorded. According to one historian, the BBC engineer on duty forgot to depress the recording needle. Others claim the BBC simply did not attach sufficient importance to the broadcast and chose not to record it. See David Schoenbrun, *Soldiers of the Night: The Story of the French Resistance* (New York: E. P. Dutton, 1980), 40-41; Don Cook, *Charles de Gaulle: A Biography* (New York: G. P. Putman's, 1983), 74-75.
10. William L. Shirer, *The Collapse of the Third Republic: An Inquiry Into the Fall of France in 1940* (New York: Simon and Schuster, 1969), 860-861.

Chapter 4
11. Robert Aron, *The Vichy Regime, 1940-1941* (New York: The Macmillan Company, 1958), 416-417; Farmer, *Vichy: Political Dilemma*, 298-299.

Chapter 5
12. By late 1943 and early 1944, Allied planes were bombing the industrial belt around Paris with increasing regularity. Factories, many of which produced German war materials, and railway yards were targeted. The Allies made every effort to avoid bombing central Paris. Thornton, *The Liberation of Paris*, 105; for specific bombing locations, see Kit C. Carter and Robert Mueller, eds., *The Army Air Forces in World War II: Combat Chronology, 1941-1945* (Washington, D.C.: Government Printing Office, 1973).
13. "In its cruelty, the *Milice* rivaled the Gestapo." John F. Sweets, *The Politics of Resistance in France, 1940-1941: A History of the Mouvements Unis de la Resistance* (DeKalb: Northern Illinois University Press, 1976), 27; Farmer, *Vichy: Political Dilemma*, 309.

Chapter 6
14. Cornelius Ryan, *The Longest Day: June 6, 1944* (New York: Simon and Schuster, 1959), 83.
15. At the time Elisabeth served in the Resistance, she knew the name of her network only as the "Donkeyman," the name designated for the unit by Major Maurice Buckmaster and the Special Operations Executive (SOE) in London (Buckmaster directed the French, or "F" section). She did not learn her network was also known as the *Reseau Jean-Marie* until after the war, when she saw her military records for the first time. The adoption of the name was most likely the work of Henri Frager, the Donkeyman's commandant who was arrested and deported to Germany a short time after Elisabeth joined the network (he was later murdered at Buchenwald). A major figure in the Buckmaster organization, Frager spent part of his time on the southern coast of France, where he worked with "Groupe Jean-Marie," a network commanded by Ange-Marie Miniconi, alias "Jean-Marie," one of the true heroes of the French Resistance. For more on Frager see M. R. D. Foot, *SOE in France: An Account of the Work of the British Special Operations Exectutive in France, 1940-1944* (London: Her Majesty's

Stationery Office, 1966). For Miniconi's role in the Resistance see Peter Leslie, *The Liberation of the Riviera: The Resistance of the Nazis in the South of France and the Story of its Heroic Leader, Ange-Marie Miniconi* (New York: Wyndham Books, 1980).

General de Gaulle sought to unite and bring under his control all the French Resistance groups. After much negotiating, in February of 1944 the Resistance "armies" were finally amalgamated, at least in principle, into a single organization: The French Forces of the Interior (FFI). General Pierre Koenig, a Gaullist, became the commander-in-chief of the FFI. On May 31, 1944, the *Maquis de l'Etang-Neuf (Yonne)* was incorporated into the FFI. See Alexander Werth, *France, 1940-1955* (New York: Henry Holt and Company, 1956), 164; Robert Bailly, *Si la Resistance m'etait . . . a travers les evenements de l'Yonne (et environs)* (Clancy: Les Presses de Imprimerie Laballery, 1990), 33.

Chapter 7

16. Charles de Gaulle, *War Memoirs*, vol. 2, *Unity, 1942-1944*, trans. Richard Howard (New York: Simon and Schuster, 1959), 256.

Chapter 8

17. Martin Blumenson, *United States Army in World War II: Breakout and Pursuit*, "The European Theater of Operations" (Washington, D.C.: Office of the Chief of Military History, Department of the Army, 1961), chapter 28 ("The Drive to the Seine").

18. On August 15, 1944, the Allied invasion of southern France began with landings between Cannes and Toulon. Code named *Anvil*, the name was changed, for security reasons, to *Dragoon* on August 1st. The landings of the newly constituted American Seventh Army were under the command of General Alexander Patch. On August 16th, the First French Army, under the command of General Jean de Lattre de Tassigny, followed with landings near Saint-Tropez. Aided by members of the French Resistance, the Allied armies were opposed by the German Nineteenth Army as they drove up the Rhône Valley toward Lyon.

The Allied High Command eagerly awaited the joining of forces from southern France (*Anvil/Dragoon*) to those driving south and east from the beaches of Normandy (*Overlord*). The consolidated Allied front would bar the escape route of the German forces in southwestern France.

The drive up the Rhône Valley went smoothly and no serious problems were encountered. Allied troops liberated Lyon on September 3rd and Dijon on September 11th. The exact time and place of the first meeting of troops from *Anvil/Dragoon* and *Overlord* is a matter of controversy. It took place no later than September 12th, when soldiers from Major General Jacques LeClerc's Second Armored Division, then attached to General Patton's Third Army, made contact with soldiers from General de Lattre's First French Army near Dijon. Advanced reconnaissance units from both armies probably met earlier, perhaps as early as September 10th. See Forest C. Pogue, *United States Army in World War II: The Supreme Command*, "The European Theater of Operations" (Washington, D.C.: Office of the Chief of Military History, Department of the Army, 1954), 227-230. See also, Robert Aron, *France Reborn: The History of the Liberation, June 1944-May 1945*, trans. Humphrey Hare (New York: Charles Scribner's Sons, 1964), 358-359; Henri Michel, *The Second World War*, vol. 2, trans. Douglas Parmee (New York: Praeger, 1975), 669-675.

Chapter 9
19. Schoenbrun, *Soldiers of the Night*, 376-388; Bailly, *Si la Resistance*, 65-66; Blake Erlich, *Resistance: France 1940-1945* (New York: Signet Books, 1965), 181.

Chapter 11
20. Michel, *The Second World War*, vol. 2, 674-681; Aron, *France Reborn*, 427-428; Pogue, *United Army in World War II: The Supreme Command*, 310-312.
21. Aron, *France Reborn*, 437-450; For a full account of *Operation Northwind*, see Charles Whiting, *The Other Battle of the Bulge: Operation Northwind*, 1st American ed. (Chelsea, MI: Scarborough House, 1990).

Chapter 13
22. Marshall de Lattre de Tassigny, *The History of the French First Army*, trans. Malcolm Barnes (London: George Allen and Unwin, Ltd., 1952), 415.

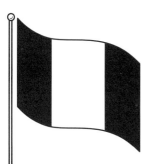

Further Reading

Aubrac, Lucie. *Outwitting the Gestapo*. Translated by Konrad Bieber. Lincoln: University of Nebraska Press, 1993.
Burrin, Philippe. *France Under the Germans: Collaboration and Compromise*. Translated by Janet Lloyd. New York: The New Press, 1996.
Churchill, Peter. *Of Their Own Choice*. London: Hodder and Stoughton, 1953.
Collins, Larry, and Dominque La Pierre. *Is Paris Burning?* New York: Simon and Schuster, 1965.
Fourcade, Marie-Madeleine. *Noah's Ark*. Translated by Kenneth Morgan. New York: E. P. Dutton, 1974.
Frenay, Henri. *The Night Will End: Memories of a Revolutionary, 1940-1943*. Translated by Dan Hofstader. New York: McGraw-Hill, 1976.
Funk, Arthur. *Hidden Ally: The French Resistance, Special Operations, and the Landings in Southern France, 1944*. New York: Greenwood Press, 1992.

Katona, Edita, and Patrick Macnaghten. *Code Name Marianne: The Autobiography of France's Most Captivating Secret Agent During World War II*. New York: David McKay Company, Inc., 1976.

Kedward, H. Roderick. *Occupied France: Collaboration and Resistance, 1940-1944*. London: Blackwell, 1985.

Rossiter, Margaret L. *Women in the Resistance*. New York: Praeger, 1986.

Ruby, Marcel. *F Section, SOE: The Buckmaster Networks*. London: Leo Cooper, 1988.

Wake, Nancy. *The Autobiography of the Woman the Gestapo Called "The White Mouse."* Melbourne: Macmillan of Australia, 1985.

Weitz, Margaret Collins. *Sisters in the Resistance: How Women Fought to Free France, 1940-1945*. New York: John Wiley & Sons, Inc., 1995.

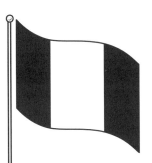

Index

by Lori L. Daniel

— A —

Adam, Jacques (Colonel), 67, 75, 129-130, 154-155
Adele, Mother, 33
Allies, xiv-xv, 11, 38, 45, 58, 66-67, 70, 77-78, 82, 86, 100-101, 105, 109, 111, 126-127, 131-132, 134
America, 50, 66, 103, 105
American, 50, 64, 66, 102, 104, 114-115, 120, 150
  army, 50
    Seventh Army, 100-101, 105
    Third Army, 77
Andre, 69, 89
Annette, 89
Armenian, xix, 3
  concentration camp, 151
Armistice, 14
Attestation, 159

— B —

Battle of France, 12
BBC (British Broadcasting Company), 58, 67
Belfort Gap, 100
Belgium, 6, 162
Blackout, 15
Boche, xiv, xix, 43, 48, 83, 125, 127
  see also German
Boot camp, 79, 93, 97, 99, 101, 106
Boyer, Henri (Lieutenant), 133-136, 138, 140, 144
Bridget, 16, 21
British, xvi, 12, 42, 91

— C —

Carpentier, Madame, 42
Catherine, 30, 35
Catholic, 1, 32, 76

Catholic *(continued)*
  Church, 103
Certificate of demobilization, 167
Certificate of Release, 168
Charles, 68-69, 71-72, 75, 78, 80-81, 139
Charlotte, 79, 113-117, 122-141, 143-145, 147, 153
CNFC *(Confederation Nationale France Combattante)*, 160
Colmar Pocket, 101, 155
Colonial Medal, 161
Combat, 53
Commemorative Medal of the Campaign of Indochina, 161
Communist, anti, 48
Crimean War, 42
Croix de Guerre, 153-154, 156
Cross of Lorraine, 158
Crusade in Europe, xv

— D —

Darnand, Joseph, 48
D-Day, 67
de Gaulle, Charles (General), 12, 64, 67, 85, 157, 162
Denise, 21-27, 47, 75, 134, 148, 155
de Tassigny, de Lattre (General), 82, 91, 100, 127
Dominique, Father, 32-33, 35
Dupond, Dr., 138, 140-141, 145-146
DuPre
  Alexander (Alex), 57, 63-65, 83-84, 86-90, 92, 96, 133, 153-154
  Anna, 87, 96, 133, 153

— E —

Eisenhower, Dwight D. (General), xv, 100
England, 12, 93
  London, 58
English, xx, 114-116, 118, 120-123, 125-127, 156, 161-162
Europe, xv, 2

— F —

Felix, 51, 53, 135-136, 138-139
First French Army, 63, 79, 82, 91, 93-94, 100-101, 105, 127
  Second Armored Division, 101
  Second Moroccan Infantry Division, 93
  First Voluntary Regiment of Yonne, 93

France, xiii-xvi, xviii-xx, xxii, 1-2, 6, 11-15, 32, 38, 48, 53, 63-64, 66-67, 75-78, 82, 92, 96, 101, 105, 118-120, 127, 135, 145, 151, 153-154, 161-162
Aix-en-Provence, 151
Alsace-Lorraine, 100, 105
Auxerre, 55, 57-58, 68-69, 71, 76-77, 79-80
Avallon, 79-80
Belfort, 79, 93, 96, 100-101
Bordeaux, 7
Bourges, 32, 34
Brittany, 77
Champagne Berrichonne, 32
  St. Mary's boarding school, 32, 34, 38-40
  Church, 32
Clermont, 13
Colmar, 79, 101, 105, 126
Compiegne, 11-12
Department of Nievre, 83
Dijon, 77, 79, 82-83, 85, 96
Ferrand, 13
Fontainebleau, 119-120
Grenoble, 84
Joigny, 146, 153
Kehl, 127
Marne, xv, xx
Marseilles, 2, 8-9, 38
Metz, 61
Montmartre, 116
Mulhouse, 101
Northern, 11
Oradour-sur-Glane, 86
Paris, xiv, xvii-xx, 1-2, 4, 6-9, 11-15, 24, 27, 29, 33-34, 39, 42-43, 45, 52, 54-55, 63, 70, 85, 110-116, 119, 122, 128, 134, 146-149, 154-155
  Arc de Triomphe, xvii, 13, 43, 117
    Tomb of the Unknown Soldier, 13, 116
  Avenue des Champs Elysées, xiii
  Avenue Simon Bolivar, 49
  Bois de Vincennes, 52
  Champs des Elysées, 44, 116
  Comedie Francaise, 117
  Gare d'Austerlitz, 43
  Gare de l'Est, 112
  Hospital Salpetriere, 43
  Hospital Tenon, 46
  Hotel des Invalides, 154
  La Madeleine, 112
  Left Bank, 43

France *(continued)*
  Paris *(continued)*
    Notre Dame, 103
    Parc des Buttes Chaumont, 1, 49
    Paris Opera, 30, 112
    Place des Voges, 115
    Ritz Hotel, 113
      USO, 113
    Rue de Belleville, 50
    Rue Rebeval, 1, 4, 50
    Rue Scribe, 112
    Scribe Hotel, 111-112
    Tenon Hospital, 155, 157
  Rhône River, 77
  Rue de l'Université, 155
  Seine River, 77
  Sens, 77
  Southeastern, 11
    see also Unoccupied Zone
  St. Germain en Laye, 1-2, 6-7, 15, 19
  Strasbourg, 79, 101, 105, 127, 132-133, 148, 153
  Third Republic, xiii, xv, 12
  Tours, 7
  University of St. Petersburg, xx
  Vercors, 84, 86
  Verdun, xv, 113
  Vichy, 12, 48-49
  Villeneuve St. Georges, 43, 84, 103, 121, 151
    Rue des Balkans, 121
Franciscan Order, 32
Free China (Formosa), 162
French, xiii-xvi, xviii, xx-xxii, 7-11, 13, 15, 21, 27, 38, 42, 47-50, 63, 67-68, 70, 72-74, 76, 85, 93, 101, 106, 108-109, 111, 114-116, 120, 122, 123, 126-129, 133, 136, 155-156, 161-162
  army, xx, 5, 63, 79, 86, 92-93, 99-101, 113, 127-128, 151, 155, 160-161
    see First French Army
  black market, 15, 24, 42
  court, 12
  government, xv, 7, 12, 160
  military police
    see Milice
  National Assembly, 12
  Resistance, xiii-xxii, 14, 48-49, 51, 54-58, 60, 62-63, 67, 70, 73, 75, 78-79, 84, 86, 88, 91-93, 98, 111, 121, 127, 133, 147, 149, 154-155, 157-160, 163
    see also Reseau Jean-Marie Resistance

French Combatants, 155

— G —

Gautier, Captain, 58-62, 64
Geoff, 56
German, xiii-xv, xvii-xxii, 2, 5-15, 20-21, 23-25, 27, 30, 38-39, 41-44, 46-50, 52-54, 56-58, 63-64, 67-78, 80-84, 86, 92, 98, 100-102, 105-106, 108-109, 111, 126-128, 132, 134-137, 139, 141
  see also Boche
  army, 1, 6, 8, 10, 105, 108
  concentration camp, 26, 34
  labor camp, xxii
  plane, 9
  SS, 49
    Das Reich, 86
  work camp, xxi
Germany, xiv, 1-2, 5, 11, 48, 68, 125-129, 131-132, 155, 162
  Berlin, xix, 20
  Black Forest, 79, 136
  Freiburg, 79, 135-137
  Karlsruhe, 79, 125, 127-128, 131-134
  Rottweil, 79, 136-137, 139
  Scheibenhardt, 127
  Ulm, 153
Gestapo, xiv, xvii, 48-49, 51, 53-54, 71, 74-75, 79, 110, 128, 147, 149
  Headquarters, 44, 47
Great Britain, 2
Greece, 94
  Larissa, 169-170

— H —

Hadjiyannis, Demetre, 170
Hitler, Adolf, 5, 8, 11, 46, 50, 105, 115, 128
Holland, 6
Holocaust, 155
Hugo, Victor, 115

— J —

Jean, 78, 84
Jean-Claude, 52-53
Jeanne d'Arc, xx, xxii, 15, 42
Jerusalem, 155
Jew, 49, 69
Jewish, 25, 44, 51, 132, 134, 151, 153, 155

— K —

Kapelian
 Annick, xix, 1, 4-5, 7-9, 15, 23, 27-31, 40-41, 45-47, 59, 89, 102, 104, 149
 Arthur, 1-2, 4-5, 38, 48, 151
 Aunt Celine, 8-10, 12, 46-47, 103
 Aunt Marthe, 102-105
 Elisabeth, xxi, 1, 5, 19, 21, 24, 26, 28, 31, 45, 54, 75, 77, 79, 93-94, 97, 107, 112, 121, 148-149, 152, 154, 158-160, 162, 164
  military records, 164-166
  see also Lisette
  see also Sevier, Elisabeth
 Grandmere, xx-xxii, 15, 84, 103-104, 121-122, 141, 151, 153
 Grandpere, xx, 15, 84, 103-104, 121-122, 141, 151, 153
 Jean (Papa), xix-xx, 1-7, 14, 34, 40, 45-48, 73, 75, 89, 102-105, 149
 Suzanne, xix, 1, 4-5, 8, 15-17, 19, 21, 23-24, 27-31, 39-42, 45-46, 48, 78, 89, 102, 104, 141, 146-149, 151-152
 Therese (Maman), xviii-xx, 1-10, 15, 17, 20-21, 23-32, 34-35, 39-43, 45-48, 50, 53-55, 75, 78, 88-89, 102-104, 111, 122, 141, 146-152, 155, 162
 Uncle Antoine, 8
 Uncle Armand, 8-10, 103
 Uncle Iria, 50

— L —

Laval, Pierre, 12
LeClerc, General, 101
Lecocq
 Lucette, 79, 98, 106, 126, 128, 132-136, 138, 140, 143-144, 146, 153
 Odette, 98, 106, 108, 110, 126, 128-129, 132, 134-135, 137-138, 144, 146, 153
Les Femmes Savantes, 117
Liberation of France, xv
Lisette, xiv-xv, 55-56, 58, 65, 78, 80, 88, 93, 96, 111, 121, 133, 143-145
 see also Kapelian, Elisabeth
 see also Sevier, Elisabeth
Louis, 69
Luftwaffe, 10
Luxembourg, 6

— M —

Madame la Directrice, 45, 53-55, 149

Maginot Line, 2, 7
Mamadou from Senegal, 136
Maquis, xiv, xxii, 58, 66, 78, 82, 86, 92, 101, 111, 163
Maquisard (Resistance fighter), 56, 59, 63, 66-69, 77-78, 82-85, 88, 155, 163
Maquis de l'Etang-Neuf (Yonne), xiv, 63, 79, 82, 93
Marie, 85-86, 56-57, 60-62, 64, 87-90
Marie (baby), 24-30, 75, 134, 148, 155
Michelle, 59-61, 79-80, 83-85, 88, 92-93, 96-98, 105-106, 108-111, 127, 139
Milice (French military police), 48-49, 71-74, 76, 81, 84, 92
Miniconi, Ange-Marie, 154
Minnesota, 121, 130
 St. Paul, 115
 University of Minnesota, 121
Moliere, ___, 117
Monique, 32-33, 35-37
Montan
 Dr., 7, 21-224, 30-31, 40, 42
 Madame, 21-23
Morse, Samuel "Sam" (Captain), 115-117, 122-124, 126, 129, 134-135

— N —

Napoleon, 120
Nazi, xiv, xviii, 12, 47, 134, 151, 153
 poster, 13-14
New Mexico State University, 162
New York
 New York City, 102, 161
Nightingale, Florence, 15, 42
Norbert, 34-37, 108
Normandy, 58, 66-67, 71, 86
North Africa, 38
North Sea, 100

— O —

Oklahoma
 Edmond, 163
 Oklahoma City, 153
O'Malley, Thomas, 65-66, 75
One Hundred Years War, xx
Operation Northwind, 105
Operation Torch, 38

— P —

Parisian, xiii, 1, 7, 9, 13-14, 27, 51-52
Patton, George S. (General), 77

Paul, Father, 34, 37
Pétain, Marshal, 11-12
   government, 12-14, 27, 38
Peters, Richard A. (Dr.), xvi, 163
Pierre, 69
Poireau, Colonel, 84-85
Poland, 1-2, 155

— R —

Randall
   Andrea, 121
   James Hubert, 115-127, 129-131, 135, 139-141, 144, 148, 150
Raynaud, Paul, 11
Red Cross, xiv, xvii, 42-44, 52-54, 56, 149
   Civil Defense identification card, 54
   Defense worker, xix
Reseau Jean-Marie Resistance, 63
Revolution, xx
Rhine River, 100-101, 106, 127
Rockefeller, John D., 120
Russia, xx

— S —

Schmidt
   Frau, 128-130, 132, 135
   Herr, 128-130, 132
Sequin, Maman, 3, 16-17, 19
Sevier
   Elisabeth Kapelian, xiv, xvi, 169-170
     see also Kapelian, Elisabeth
     see also Lisette
   Robert W. "Bob," 161-162
Sister Louise, 16-18
Sisters of Mercy, 161
Sister Veronica, 16-17
Sobel, Madame, 27-29
Song
   "*Besame Mucho*," 114-115
   "Goodnight Sweetheart," 115
   "Silent Night," 105
   "Song of Autumn," 58

Song *(continued)*
   "The Hymn of the Resistance," xii
Soutille, Dr., 56, 61-62, 64-66, 80, 85, 87, 89, 91, 111, 130, 135, 155, 161
Spanish, 161
Stowe, Harriet Beecher, 103
Switzerland, 100-101

— T —

Texas, 123
   El Paso, 161, 163
     Hotel Dieu Hospital, 161
     University of Texas, 161
   Fort Bliss, 161
   Houston, 115
   Junction, 153
The Last of the Mohicans, 104
Tulle executions, 86

— U —

Uncle Tom's Cabin, 103
United States, 131, 151, 161
   Army, 91, 161
Unoccupied Zone, 11, 12, 27, 32, 38
   see also Southeastern France

— V —

Verlaine, Paul, 58
Victor, 21-27, 47, 75, 134, 148, 155
Vietnam, 155, 161

— W —

Wolfgang, 108
World War I, xix, 11, 151
World War II, xxii, 114, 158, 168

— Y —

Yom HaShoah (Holocaust Remembrance), 155
Yves, 139
Yvonne, 3

Other World War II Titles
from
Sunflower University Press®

PASSAGES TO FREEDOM: A Story of Capture and Escape, by Joseph S. Frelinghuysen. 2nd Printing.

WE DELIVERED! The U.S. Navy Armed Guard in World War II, by Lyle E. Dupra.

A WARRIOR FOR FREEDOM: Admiral Robert B. Carney, by Betty Carney Taussig.

CAMP CONCORDIA: German POWs in the Midwest, by Lowell A. May.

BROTHERS FROM BATAAN: POWs, 1942-1945, by Adrian R. Martin.

BAIL-OUT! POW, 1944-1945, by Mel TenHaken.

THE MAN OF CONFIDENCE: A Greek POW in World War II, by Anastasios Aslanis.

FIGHTER PILOT — World War II in the South Pacific, by William M. Gaskill.

Complete backlist and brochure available:
800-258-1232